P9-DVA-683

Women's Running

Women's Running

by Joan Ullyot, M.D.

cover photo: Lorraine Rorke

Recommended Reading:
Runner's World Magazine, $9.50/year
Write for a free catalog of publications
and supplies for runners and other athletes.

© 1976 by
World Publications
P.O. Box 366, Mountain View, CA 94042
No information in this book may be reprinted in any
form without permission from the publisher.
Library of Congress 75-20962
ISBN 0-89037-100-8 (Hb.) — 0-89037-073-7 (Pb.)
Second Printing, November 1976
Third Printing, May 1977
Fourth Printing, June 1977
Fifth Printing, October 1977

Contents

Foreword 3

PART ONE: TRAINING PLANS

Principles. 6
Beginners. 10
Intermediates 25
Racers. 34
Schedules 50

PART TWO: AIDS AND ADVICE

Shoes. 62
Clothing 68
Diet. 72
Safety 85

PART THREE: RUNNING MEDICINE

Physiology. 88
Fat as Fuel 91
Injuries 97
Treatment. 103
Other Questions 117

PART FOUR: THE RESULTS

1974 "International" 132
1975 "National". 141

APPENDIX

Basic Fitness Test 150
Women's Time Standards 150
Race Pacing Tables 151
Mile-Meter Conversions. 152
Metric Pacing Tables 153
Recommended Reading. 154
About the Author 155

Dedicated with thanks

To the five Compleat Runners whose experience and friendship have greatly influenced my own running and thoughts about running . . .

> *Dr. Ernst van Aaken*
> *Ron Daws*
> *Joe Henderson*
> *Dr. George Sheehan*
> *Walt Stack*

and to my husband, Dr. Dan Ullyot, who stood by me during my unexpected transformation from creampuff to marathoner.

Foreword

I recently read a quotation from the renowned heart surgeon, Dr. Christian Bernard, a slim, energetic man who professes to scorn physical exercise.

He said, "Exercise is like a cold bath — you hate it when you're taking it and you're happy when it's over. I'd rather avoid it altogether."

I, too, hate exercise. I have dismal memories of high school gym classes, where we stood around the field waiting for a turn at bat, or did brisk calisthenics on the lawn. College gym class was worse. We dragged ourselves out of bed early in the morning so as not to miss compulsory class, in which we practiced total body relaxation while lying on the cold gym floor.

"You are feeling very heavy," the gym teacher would intone as two-thirds of the class went off to sleep again.

Later in life, conscious of admonitions that "exercise is good for you," I periodically tackled the Royal Canadian Air Force Physical Fitness program, dutifully bobbing to touch my toes, flinging my arms around for the prescribed 10-12 minutes daily. I was bored to death and would drop the program quietly after a few weeks — first one day would be neglected, then two, then a whole week.

This pattern is not unusual — in fact, it is normal for "exercise programs," and it points out one crucial fact. Most people regard exercise as an unpleasant duty and do it only as an act of will power. I am no different, except that my will power may be weaker than others.

So why do I now run almost every day of the year, in rain, snow and heat waves? Not to get my daily exercise, I assure you. *Only* because I love running.

This is the key. You aren't going to do any exercise unless you love it and discover you're not a whole person without it. You have to experience not only the physical well-being and energy that come from being fit, but also the genuine pleasure of moving your body actively. The exhilaration one can experience from running is similar to the high felt by skiers on a fresh powder slope or surfers when riding a wave.

This is not "exercise." This is living to one's fullest capacity. All the health benefits of exercise are peripheral to this euphoria. They do come, but just as gravy to add on the main dish. They are not the *reason* for doing it. They are a pleasant bonus.

Joan Ullyot, M.D.
San Francisco, Calif.
April 1976

Part I

Training Plans

one

Principles

There are no great secrets to training for long-distance running. The general principles are very simple — (1) adaptation to overload (stress) and (2) consistency.

The idea is to stress your body slightly beyond its current capabilities. The natural response is for the body to become stronger to meet the stress. You then stress it again at a slightly lighter level and the body adapts further.

Consistency — virtually *daily* running — is necessary or the body lapses back to its former state and all that work of adaptation has been in vain. So it's wise not to let yourself get unfit again, especially if the initial stages of acquiring fitness have been painful for you. Who would want to go through that again? Get in the habit of taking a pair of running shoes with you on vacation, business trips, and so forth. That way, you'll never be unequipped to get in the little bit of training necessary at least to maintain your condition.

Since the concept of training is so simple, it apalls me that I managed to reach age 30, to graduate from medical school and go through countless years of gym classes in school and college without having the faintest inkling of the body's potential for athletic development. I had the vague idea that you were born with certain talents such as being able to run a five-minute mile or being able to swim fast — and that was that. Sure, I knew that it took practice to learn to ride a bike, play the piano or to hit a golf or tennis ball. But this sort of eye-hand coordination and skill was not associated in my mind with athletics. I was decidedly unathletic.

Looking back now, I realize my abysmal ignorance. Once, at age 12, I spent a summer in the water — swimming, playing, practicing for a life-saving course. I swam for hours daily. At the end of the summer, there was a one-mile race across the lake, which I entered most reluctantly. The lake was fed by melting snow and was frigid at the 5 a.m. starting time.

My astonishment was profound when I swam the lake more than 10 minutes faster than the previous year. I did not connect this feat with my daily swimming workout, but only felt vaguely that perhaps some native talent of mine had emerged suddenly.

Years later I had trouble keeping up with my husband on our rare weekend hikes (never more than 5-7 miles) and got quite used to trailing several hundred yards behind. Our dog would return anxiously every so often to make sure I was still there.

On moving to California, we were closer to the outdoors and started hiking most weekends. Again, I was astonished after several months to find I was hiking farther and no longer trailing. I still didn't make the connection nor realize I actually was increasing my aerobic capacity by training. I got into physical condition by pure accident, and my comprehension of what was happening lagged far behind the changes in my body.

Nowadays, thanks to such best-selling books on training as Dr. Kenneth Cooper's *Aerobics* or Bill Bowerman's *Jogging*, it is to be hoped that no one remains in such depths of ignorance. Certainly any woman can make faster progress than I did by knowing what she's doing and have more fun in the process.

After I had been jogging a mile 2-3 times a week, I found I not only enjoyed the exercise but also was beginning to run my mile faster and more easily. I discovered Cooper's *Aerobics* and began to learn about the fantastic process of adaptation that was going on throughout my body (in the heart, lungs, blood and muscles, not to mention my head).

It is important to remember that a given amount of consistent training will result in fairly predictable progress. Results cannot be seen as day-to-day improvements in speed or

The training must fit the activity. Fitness runners can't train like these young cross-country racers.

Jeff Johnson

fitness, but seem to appear in steps. At each stage you'll reach a plateau, then make a sudden jump and do much better than before. For this reason, it is unwise to time yourself daily. Every few weeks is perfectly adequate if you're interested in recording your progress. And if you're jogging for health reasons, not for improvement, enjoy the runs and don't even bother timing them.

The discussion in this book is divided into three sections, so you can skip to the one which matches your level.

- *Beginners:* self-explanatory (see pages 10-24).

- *Intermediates:* For those who can run 2-3 miles or 20-30 minutes comfortably and would like to progress further. This section includes information on low-key road racing (see pages 25-33).

- *Racers:* For experienced road runners who would like to race faster or tackle a marathon (see pages 35-60).

Certain principles apply at all stages. The most important of these are:

1.   *Regularity.* Daily activity is necessary for progress. However, each day's session need not be long or hard.

2. *"Hard/easy" pattern.* The body responds best to a stressful (hard) workout if it is given a chance to recuperate and consolidate its gains the following day. The easy day may vary from rest or a walk in the beginning stage to a comfortably paced 3-6 miles at later levels.

3. *Distance over speed.* At all stages of training, the time will come when formerly hard workouts don't seem much more of an effort than walking the dog around the block. You'll want to do more to get that good feeling of exertion. It's better to increase your effort by extending the distance run — slow your pace if necessary — than trying to run a set distance faster. This is because *endurance* is the necessary base for all running and by going longer, you will automatically find you are training to go faster as well. The reverse is not the case since it is easy to have speed over short distances without developing any stamina.

two

Beginners

If you are a beginner and are reading this book, chances are you have a friend or husband or both who runs and you are wondering if you should try it yourself. Motives for starting vary widely, but usually involve a wish to improve one's health, to acquire and increase stamina, to eliminate middle-aged spread, to improve conditioning for other sports such as tennis, to ward off heart disease or to stop smoking.

Be of good cheer. Running will indeed help you in all of these ways, and for a minimal investment of both time and money: 15-20 minutes daily, and one $20-30 pair of running shoes.

Though almost everyone starts running for reasons of health, very few keep on with it for such reasons. As one becomes fit, the motivation slowly changes to self-gratification. One runs because it feels good, plain and simple.

I'm always amused when non-runners express amazement at my daily running and admire my supposedly tremendous will power which enables me to drive myself so hard. Actually, I have very little will power and am basically a hedonist. I wouldn't run if I didn't like it. In fact, if I take more than a few days off now, I have physical withdrawal symptoms like any addict — headaches, nervousness (bitchiness, my husband elaborates helpfully), insomnia and constipation. I plunge back into running with tremendous relief and an exhilaration "high."

This high is a common phenomenon among distance runners. I mention it now because as you go through the initial phase of conditioning — achieving basic training — you'll have to push yourself through some painful periods. It helps to know that it won't always be that way.

As soon as you can jog a mile steadily and comfortably, or as soon as you can take your mind off what your feet are doing, you can begin to enjoy the scenery and smells, the chat or the time for relaxation. Then you'll begin to notice a surge of energy and exhilaration *after* the run.

The final stage of enjoyment is when you're fit, no longer puffing or straining for breath or wincing from muscle or joint pains. Then you'll find you enjoy the run itself, the breeze in your hair, the smooth motion of arms and legs, the sensation of gliding along, the joy of movement. Then you're hooked. Welcome to the society of running "nuts."

Even for those who have run before, this feeling may be new. In my first years of running, my husband, a 440-yard dash specialist in high school, couldn't understand why I ran. I tried to explain in the terms I just used.

He frowned and cross-examined me. "Let me get this straight, Joan. Do you mean to say you actually get some sort of *physical pleasure* out of running?"

Blushing and feeling as if I were confessing some perversion, I admitted to it.

"Then you're not doing it right," he snapped. "You have to run harder!"

That, I have since learned, is the typical advice of the 440 runner for whom training is agony and the only reward is faster times. It took weeks of enjoyable, aerobically paced running with me ("Do you always run this slow?" he would ask) to convert him to the pleasure principle. But now he, too, runs regularly and enjoys it.

SAFETY PRECAUTIONS

If you are over 40 years of age or if you have any health problems such as diabetes, a heart murmur or a history of rheumatic fever, it is important to check with a doctor before starting any new, vigorous exercise. If you have been a smoker, it is doubly important. This is because as smoking and stress increase among women so do their chances of developing coronary artery disease (CAD) — narrowing of the coronary arteries that supply blood to the heart muscle itself. Occlusion of one or more of these arteries can cause chest pain (angina), heart attack or even sudden death.

Factors that increase one's risk of CAD include cigarette smoking, high blood pressure, a family history of heart attacks, sedentary habits, stress and overweight. Your own doctor is best qualified to judge if you fall into the high risk group. If so, he may recommend a "stress EKG" (see medical section, page 126-127) in addition to a regular resting EKG, which by itself gives little information about the state of the coronary arteries.

If you are under 40, or older but reasonably fit and active (for instance, if you hike, play tennis, swim or bike regularly) you undoubtedly will get medical clearance. The mild to moderate stress imposed on the heart during jogging actually is less than that involved in more strenuous but intermittent sports like tennis. So if you already know your heart is up to the challenge, there is no need to check it out further.

HOW TO START

First, get yourself a good pair of training shoes. Your comfortable old Hush Puppies, sneakers, desert boots or tennis specials, no matter how expensive, *won't* do. (See Chapter 6 on shoes). Besides, investing up to $30 in a pair of shoes helps keep you going through the first weeks. You'll want to get your money's worth.

Then, dressed in the new shoes and some comfortable clothes — any clothes — go out and run a bit. At this stage, you should find a place which is as flat and scenic as possible. If you live on a beautiful, suburban, tree-lined street, you can start right at your front door. Otherwise, find a nearby park, golf course or track.

Generally, I don't recommend tracks because running around them can be extremely dull. But if there's nothing better, a track will do. Run for a distance of, for instance, two miles. More than that, eight laps, will drive most people nuts and they soon become ex-joggers, saying, "Running? I tried it once but I got bored."

Someone has said that it's hard to get into trouble running, as long as you remember to alternate feet. Try to land flat footed or heel first and not on your toes because that is only for sprinters. Jog at a comfortable speed, defined as one at which you can breathe normally and talk. If you're with a friend, chat as you jog. Otherwise, mumble or hum to yourself. If you have enough breath left for talking, you won't be over-straining yourself.

Wear a watch and aim for 10-15 minutes or one mile daily for the first week. Don't think you have to jog the entire time. Generally, only women under 30, or those already fairly fit from other activities, can run a mile non-stop. The rest will be out of breath and stop talking after 100 yards to a quarter of a mile or no more than 2-3 minutes.

When this happens, walk until your breathing is comfortable again, then jog as before. Repeat until the time (or mile) is up. As the days go by, you'll find yourself jogging farther until you're finally fit enough to run 15 minutes non-stop.

For most women in their 30s and 40s who are initially unfit, this takes about two weeks. If you're overweight or a smoker or older, it will be longer. But you *will* make it eventually, if you train regularly (a minimum of every other day but preferably five days a week at this stage).

When you can jog a mile, or 10-15 minutes, non-stop, don't try to go faster. Instead, extend the distance to two miles (about 20 minutes), slowing the pace a bit if necessary to make up for the longer effort. At the end of the 1-3 months (usually longer if you're over 50), you'll be running comfortably for two miles or more and can go on to the intermediate section if you wish.

I'm often asked how much running is necessary. It depends on what your goals are. If you wish to keep in good physical condition (better condition than 95% of American women) and have an enjoyable daily routine, just stick with the 20-30 minutes or 2-3-mile program. This is all you need to be glowing with health and have many of the benefits of running. It's not the amount you do but the regularity that's important.

I'd like to see every man, woman and child in America run his or her two miles daily just as routinely as they brush their teeth. This would eliminate a lot of problems that result from the sedentary life — boredom, tension, violence, that old bugaboo constipation, dependence on tranquilizers, cigarettes and other drugs. Utopia could be found for less than 30 minutes per day!

The only reason to run more, in my opinion, is if you want the psychological high that often is most noticeable in longer runs, or if you wish to explore your capabilities, to test yourself against your own physiology and against others by racing. Some running doctors believe that in order to ward off coronary artery disease, it is necessary to jog six miles or one hour daily rather than just 20 minutes. As yet, there is no real evidence to support this belief, and anyone who prefers to jog about an hour a day, in my opinion, should do so because she enjoys the hour's activity and not out of fear of heart disease.

EARLY OBSTACLES

The aches and pains that can accompany beginning running — sprained ankles, sore muscles and shin splints — are discussed later in the medical section (pages 103-116).

There are other more subtle problems that may interfere with the early running program and result in discouragement or failure before fitness is achieved and running becomes self-perpetuating. Chief among these problems are self-consciousness, boredom and well-meaning but misguided advice and help from others.

Almost every woman feels self-conscious during her first runs. In most parts of the US, women joggers are not yet a common sight. The exception may be California.

At the beginning, it helps to run with a female friend and go to a track or park where there are lots of other runners and you don't feel conspicuous. Don't worry about making a faux-pas at the track. Anything goes, but generally stay out of the innermost lane (preserved for meets) and watch out for footballs, frisbees and discuses if you use the grass inside the track. Run clockwise if you prefer it to the usual counter-clockwise direction of other runners.

I remember my first run (this was in 1971). It was dusk and I went to jog a mile (I hoped) with a friend, another woman doctor in her 30s. Though we headed for a park which was running turf for many men, I had never seen a woman run and felt acutely self-conscious, as did my friend. We had the feeling everyone passing us in a car was staring, pointing and whispering about us—though in retrospect I'm sure no one even noticed us. I tried to look as small and inconspicuous as possible (I'm 5'9" tall) by wearing an old pair of nondescript blue jeans that blended into the dusk and a grey turtleneck pullover that I pulled over my chin to prevent me from being recognized.

Then I started to jog and had other things to think about — like keeping going. My friend and I muttered words of encouragement to each other. Endless steps later, we completed the mile. We were so elated we jabbered enthusiastically all the way back to the locker room and didn't even notice if others were around, much less worry about their staring.

In weeks to come, when I often ran alone, I did hear some isolated remarks — not always polite — from passing motorists. But by then I had acquired the ultimate defense against self-consciousness — namely, smugness and a "fitter than thou" attitude. (Poor slobs, I'd think, as they drove past in their big cars, smoking cigarettes and getting fatter all the time. They are envious of me because I'm healthy and enjoying myself.)

With that attitude, no one can make you feel self-conscious.

BOREDOM

After giving a talk on the joys of running, I'm frequently approached by ex-joggers (usually men, as I recall) who maintain that they tried once or twice but stopped because they found it boring. I'm always inclined to think they haven't been doing it right because I am never bored when I run. But then I realize that I take definite precautions to avoid the possibility of boredom.

Any repetitive activity can seem dull and purposeless. For me, swimming laps in a pool is this way. For others, it may be putting one foot in front of another, day after day, mile after mile. There is no doubt that many who start jogging with enthusiasm *do* drop out because of "boredom." On questioning, they usually show a definite pattern of running.

● *Monotony.* They run the same distance daily, or the same time. And always on the same track or road, with little scenic interest.

● *Speed fixation.* Frequently, the main interest of the run, for these people, lies in the time it takes. They try to go faster over their monotonous route every day. Improvement is rapid at first, as they get into condition, but then it slows. They may even do worse from one day to the next — we all have our ups and downs — and this can be discouraging if you're obsessed with speed. Result: "boredom."

● *Lack of company.* Being concerned with speed rather than scenery or talk (which cuts down on speed), these people usually run alone and frequently rehash the day's problems during their self-prescribed "exercise time."

This type of running is what Dr. Meyer Friedman has in mind when he declares, in his book *Type A Behavior and the Heart,* that running is the worst thing you can do and tends to intensify "Type A Behavior," which is time-oriented, compulsive activity. I agree. But people who run this way rarely stick with it for long because of boredom.

To avoid boredom, to the extent where you never notice it, simply eliminate the factors of monotony, speed fixation and lack of company. Choose scenic, varied routes. Even the same route backwards can look new and different. Don't be concerned with the distance run, so you don't have to stick to known, measured routes on tracks.

Run with friends whenever possible. Talk, smell the flowers, enjoy the weather. And don't run so fast that all you can think about is getting enough air into your lungs and keeping your aching legs moving. If you forget about speed, you may find yourself going out for a 15-minute jog on a new route and having a half-hour go by before you notice it. You won't be bored.

In our beginning running groups, I have found that it's usually the men who have problems with boredom rather than the women. Perhaps they are brought up to be more time-oriented and compulsive. They often feel they have to prove their masculinity by running fast and it takes a bit of persuasion to get them to enjoy themselves and run slower, with the group. Women don't have this speed-machismo hangup, and are seldom "bored by running," in my experience.

HUSBANDS

Husbands or boyfriends can be either a great help or hindrance to beginning runners. Obviously, if your husband disapproves of your running, calls it unfeminine, teases you, complains about your sweaty clothes, scoffs at your achievements, you will have hard going. You'll probably end up either divorced or a non-runner.

Fortunately, most husbands try to help. Many are themselves runners and are delighted when you join them and can *really* understand, finally, their own passion for the sport. I've noticed that almost all male road runners share this delightful attitude toward women who run. They are pleased to be joined by us and are full of helpful advice and encouragement.

But back to the man who shares your home — and, I hope, your enthusiasm. He may wish to run with you and guide your initial steps. Say no. Pleasant as it may be to have company, it is unwise to run with a man until you are reasonably fit and can run under 10 minutes per mile.

One of the sad facts of life is that even a paunchy, beer drinking, smoking, middle-aged slob, if he's male, can almost always run a mile faster and more easily without practice than a woman. It's discouraging for you and can lead to understandable feelings of resentment if you set out together. It's unjust, but there it is — your horribly unfit husband is a better miler than you at the start.

If your husband is in good shape, you'll understand and tolerate his better performance. But he will have trouble going as slowly as you *must* in your conditioning stage. He will have to jog circles around you, chatter incessantly to use up his excess wind, sprint ahead now and then to stretch his legs. You will feel like a plodder, slow and snail-like, and soon will feel guilty about slowing him down.

Actually, since the pace you'll be going is right for you, you should stick with it and not try to speed up or push too much to keep up with your well-meaning husband. It's much better to go alone or with some woman friends. The danger of injury or overstress is less and the mental outlook much more upbeat.

Later on, when you can do your two miles comfortably and have progressed to the intermediate stage, by all means accept your husband's offer of company. When you can keep up, chat as you run, and have enough experience not to be lured into a too-fast pace, it's fun to run together.

A related problem, which often occurs at the later stages of conditioning, and with husbands who used to run track, is that of the husband-coach complex. A husband can progress from a patronizing attitude toward your early steps to pride in your achievements, toward enthusiasm and ambition.

"If you just do a little interval work, dear," he may say, "a few 440s and 220s, you'll really get good and we'll see how fast you can run a mile."

He may even develop a dangerous gleam in his eyes as he mentions the upcoming Olympics.

I would agree that at later stages a little speed work can be invaluable. And you may, in fact, develop it into a champion runner if that's your ambition. But I'm doubtful that a husband is the right person to supervise this program, any more than he should teach his wife to drive or hit a golf ball.

There have been several successful women runners coached by their husbands. Cheryl Bridges and Judy Ikenberry are two examples. But in these cases, the coach became the husband rather than vice versa. The instructor-student relationship *preceded* the marriage. Most women, even those who are

married to outstanding runners, find it better to follow their
own training program without direct supervision by their
husbands. Running is a sport which encourages independence
and self-sufficiency.

UNSOLICITED ADVICE

There must be something appealing and helpless about a
woman out jogging alone. Males standing by the sidewalk will
frequently eye you sympathetically and say "attagirl" or "right
on" by way of encouragement. Sometimes they try to be
helpful as well. "Lift your knees," they'll say, or "Land on your
toes, honey." They are wrong. Pay no attention. See the
following section on style.

Male joggers rarely receive such unsolicited advice for some
reason, nor do women offer it. I think many "sidewalk
coaches" feel that because they are men, they naturally know
more about running than women. But unless they themselves
are distance runners, this is a false assumption. So if someone
tries to correct your "style" or tell you how to run, just smile
sweetly and turn a deaf ear.

Ironically, beginning male runners seem to have more
serious style faults than women. You often can recognize the
novice runner at a distance — the high-bounding gallop, the long
stride and the forceful landing and take off are all characteristic.
These men may charge past you, working and sweating hard,
breathing heavily, wearing sneakers and a slightly contemptuous
look. Don't be tempted to imitate them, or you too will be
limping around painfully for days to come. First-time male runners often pound along swiftly for a mile or two then are forced
to walk. You may very well shuffle past them again before the
end of your own run.

STYLE

The best natural runners are young girls who are not biased
by football hero-worship and therefore do not try to imitate
sprinters. Doing what comes naturally, you will automatically
develop your own most efficient and relaxed way of running as
you put in the miles and as the distance you run becomes

Husbands are good company but poor coaches says Joan Ullyot, running here with husband Dan.

longer. Each person has her own distinctive natural style and carriage, and style per se has little influence on running capabilities.

There are certain basics to keep in mind when you start
(again, watch the young girls for a model). Try to land
flat-footed or heel first so that each stride is cushioned. Only
sprinters run on their toes. Their speed is greater but so is the
stress on leg muscles. If you run this way for more than a
quarter-mile, you set yourself up for shin-splints.

Arms should be relaxed and kept rather low. I've noticed
some women jogging along with hands clutched tightly to the
chest beneath the breasts. Perhaps they are trying to keep their
bust from bouncing too much (get a better bra if this is a
problem) or perhaps they are just tense. But if you hold your
arms tightly and don't allow them to sway naturally to counter
the motion of the legs, you'll find your shoulders are rotating
instead, leading to inefficient motion. Shake your shoulders and
arms loose now and then as you jog, to make sure they're
relaxed.

One other style fault seems more frequent in women than
in men. This is bringing the foot forward by swinging it out to
the side rather than by raising the knee. Perhaps it is a hangover
from the days of wearing tight skirts. Remember, the knee joint
is designed to act as a hinge, not a swivel. You needn't
exaggerate the knee lift. High knee lift is vital for sprinters as it
extends the stride, but is hard on the muscles of long-distance
runners and unnecessary. Just lift the knees enough so your feet
can move back and forth in a straight line and you won't
expend energy sideways.

Watch your footprints if you run along the beach
sometime and you should see your steps falling along a straight,
narrow line. As the body balances on each foot in succession,
the hips must naturally swing to keep your center of gravity
over the foot. Since most women have a slightly wider distance
between their hip joints than men, this hip swing will be more
pronounced in the women. Their gait may be fractionally less
efficient than a man's. It is not a style fault, but a natural
motion.

The style of men and women distance runners moving at
the same pace is remarkably similar. As the pace quickens, the

stride naturally lengthens slightly, arm action is more pronounced and the runner tends to land more on the toes. At
slower paces, most runners have a more shuffling gait, with a
shorter and lower stride. These adaptations to different speeds
occur naturally and you needn't think about them.

The most efficient running posture is upright. Leaning
forward won't make you go any faster. It will just strain your
thighs as your legs work to keep you from falling on your face.

Finally, don't bounce or spring into the air with each step
as do the male beginners who may charge past you, showing off.
Any upward motion is just as wasted as sideways or backwards
motion. Save your energy for going forward.

WEATHER

Sooner or later, the day will come when there's a torrent
of rain outside your window. In the early stages, you'll
probably feel relieved and say, "Oh good, I won't have to run
today." But what if it rains (or snows) for days on end? Before
you know it, in just a few days, that hard-earned conditioning
will be down the drain and you'll be out of the budding running
habit.

Better to go out for your mile or two, no matter what the
weather. After all, you're going to shower afterwards. Why not
get soaked first?

Once you're in better shape, you'll find running in the rain
not at all unpleasant (as long as it's not cold and windy as well).
The drizzle or rain feels nice on your face and you can enjoy
fresh smells and the solitude. Also, you'll feel smug about doing
something for your body while everyone else stays indoors or
inside a car, just sitting around.

Living in California, I've only had to run in the snow once,
but that was also nice. I had to pick my feet up and lift my
knees higher than usual, and when I didn't watch out going
around corners I'd slip and fall, but softly, thanks to the snow.

I know several women marathoners (and many more men)
who train successfully through the bitter Minnesota winters —
sub-zero temperatures, ice, sleet and so forth. There is plenty of

griping about the lousy weather, but these women manage to get in 60-80 miles per week and are in excellent shape for the Boston Marathon come April. So it *can* be done.

Remember, too, that in snow you can always substitute a cross-country ski excursion for your daily run, if you'd prefer. The physiological effect is comparable.

WARMUP

The purpose of the warmup is to ease your muscles — including that most important muscle, the heart — gently into the more vigorous demands of exercise. In the case of skeletal muscles, gentle walking and jogging actually does increase blood flow to the active muscles and thus warms them up. A warm muscle is more relaxed and supple, thus less likely to stiffen up and be strained or torn by sudden movement.

Obviously, the faster the run contemplated, the more important it is to warm up. Sprinters preparing for the 100-yard dash should devote a half hour or more to the warmup. Even so, they are very susceptible to pulled muscles because of the tremendous tension placed on the legs during a few seconds.

If you are just going out for an easy jog, you can incorporate the warmup into your run. Just take the first few minutes very slow and easy. You may prefer to jog and walk for five minutes. It is also helpful to do gentle stretching exercises such as toe touching and hamstring stretching before you start to run. Try to ease gently into the stretched position and hold it there, but don't push to the point of pain and don't bounce or jerk as you were probably taught back in some gym class. Bouncing just causes a reflex contraction of the stretched muscles and increases tension within the fibers.

The second aim of the warmup is to give your heart a chance to adjust to a higher workload before you send it racing up to a near-maximum (something it is best to avoid anyway). This situation should only occur before a race, which involves a fast start. One study of a group of middle-aged men showed that if they began running without warming up, a large percentage had temporary EKG changes — premature or "ectopic" beats or even some signs of transient ischemia. These signals of a heart in mild distress could be eliminated by a brief warmup.

As a rough rule of thumb, the older you are, the less fit or the faster you plan to start out, the more important it is to warm up properly. Paavo Nurmi, who won the 1500-meter and 5000-meter runs in the 1924 Olympics, both in world record times, warmed up for three hours before the race. His muscles undoubtedly appreciated it.

three

Intermediates

There are many valid reasons for extending one's daily run, ranging from the philosophical to the practical. You should realize, however, that if your goal is to keep in shape, there is really no physical reason to do more than two miles per day. Some would even say that 12 minutes is adequate.

One study of joggers at the University of California in Berkeley showed no measurable difference in maximal oxygen uptake between those who ran 12 minutes a day, three times a week, and another group which exercised twice as long for each session. All improved in fitness to about the same extent.

Of course, a longer period of training — measured in years rather than weeks — could have given different results, as might other measurements of progress — say in relaxation, euphoria or even possible future resistance to heart disease. But the most universally accepted measurement of cardiorespiratory fitness — the maximal oxygen uptake — was not affected by doubling the running time. By that standard alone, you can get fit in 12 minutes a day — or 36 minutes per week — as so many books promise but few deliver.

Why, then, are you reading this section on "the intermediate"? Why do you want to progress beyond the level of fitness you have achieved already? There are probably as many different answers as there are readers. I only can give a few of my own reasons — because I, too, started running to lose my "middle-aged spread" and, incidentally, to become "fit" according to Dr. Kenneth Cooper's tables.

Once these goals were achieved — after a couple of months

— I too kept on extending my limits beyond the known territory. In part, this was a journey of exploration. It was such a new thing for me to achieve any sort of physical ability that I was curious to see how much farther I could go. I'm still curious and still pushing back my limits. It's a fascinating search that I hope will go on indefinitely. Probably when I'm 80, I'll still be exploring, wondering just how much an 80-year-old lady who has been jogging for 50 years can still expect from her body.

On a less philosophical plane, it seems silly to spend 10-15 minutes changing and 20 minutes showering when you're only out running for a mile or two. Might as well go longer, as long as you're there.

I've also noticed that no matter what the average daily training stint — one mile, three miles or 10 — there always comes the time when your body adjusts, is in harmony with the work load and no longer feels stressed. It's odd, but true, that you can run a fairly brisk five miles and feel quite full of energy afterward — almost, one might say, unexercised. When that time comes, it's natural to increase the workload slightly, so you still feel you've "had a workout" that day and have the exhilaration that comes from pushing your body to new heights.

If there's an informal running club in your area that sponsors weekend races, there's a whole new world open to you. It's fun to test yourself now and then against others, and against your own past capabilities. Generally, after the first few races, you'll find yourself surrounded by a "peer-group" — mostly other women, older or heavier men, lots of children — all of about your own abilities. The rest of the runners are ignored, in practice. They are either far ahead or far behind. You'll find that only your peer-group position matters to you and provides a gauge of how you're progressing.

SOCIAL RUNNING

This phenomenon may have its highest development on the west coast, where runners need never be alone. They say that if you draw a chalk line across any street in California, 100 runners immediately will appear out of the bushes, ready for a race. Many running clubs are family-oriented and sponsor picnics, Easter egg hunts, skating parties or potluck dinners, when they're not organizing runs.

Such clubs obviously are a great incentive to intermediate runners. While it's pleasant to get in your half-hour run daily, just because it makes you feel good, there's added spice if you're running with a particular goal in mind, like setting a "personal best" time in the big race around the lake.

If there's no running club in your area, you might consider starting one. The most successful association of running nuts in California, the San Francisco Dolphin-South End Runners, sponsors informal weekend races whenever there's a gap in the more serious AAU schedule. Races are usually from 3-5 miles, thus ideal for the intermediate. All finishers get ribbons and club members earn points based on miles run in races. Hundreds of trophies are passed out at year's end, based on the point totals accumulated. Competition is fierce for the top trophies, but speed is irrelevant. So the oldest or slowest members have the same chance as the club hot-shots — perhaps more since the hot-shots may injure themselves and drop down in point totals. Appropriately, the club's emblem is a turtle, and the DSE motto is, "Start slowly and then ease off."

San Francisco may have more women marathoners than any other part of the US. More than 20 qualified for the Boston Marathon in 1976 by running better than 3:30 for the 26.2 miles. These Bay Area women are not superhuman. They simply benefit from a well-organized progression of training.

Starting as 2-3-mile joggers, for the usual variety of reasons, they soon "run into" other women on their daily runs and learn about the shorter DSE races. Once hooked on these weekend fun-races, with their ebullient party atmosphere, the budding competitor starts running longer in daily runs and enters the longer (six miles and up) AAU races. After a year or two, noticing that all their friends are going off to marathons here and there, they feel the urge to try it themselves, just out of curiosity. And then the personal challenge takes hold again.

All along the way, training is made easier because of the

large number of fellow runners who plan scenic runs, cross-country workouts followed by picnics or Sunday runs-with-brunch. Runners *do* eat a lot, but usually in conjunction with a social run so they feel virtuous rather than simply gluttonous.

SOURCES OF INFORMATION

What if you live in the middle of North Dakota or Nebraska, or any area where joggers rarely appear on the horizon? What if you're not just the first but the only one in your neighborhood, or your town, to run on the roads? There'll be no experienced person to ask for help or advice. Fortunately, there are national groups and publications you'll find helpful.

The National Jogging Association (1910 K St., N.W., Washington, D.C. 20006) has members across the country and sends a newsletter, advice, books, shoes, etc., to members. Dues are $10 a year, a bargain.

Road Runners Clubs of America, an association of clubs and individuals eager to help running and promote the sport with a minimum of hassle, may be able to tell you about groups in your area. (The national RRCA co-president is Jeff Darman, 2737 Devonshire Place, N.W., Washington, D.C. 20008). The European equivalent, Spiridon, sponsors races in France, Germany, Switzerland and other countries. You can join in on your vacation.

Runner's World, an informative and interesting monthly magazine, is published by World Publications, Box 366, Mountain View, Calif. 94040. Subscriptions are $9.50 per year. You also can obtain from the publisher almost all the books listed in the appendix under "Recommended Reading."

TRAINING FOR SHORT ROAD RACES

Up to this point in "the making of a runner," you can follow your nose in training. Listen to your body, run regularly, run gently (aerobically) and you'll become fit — and faster. But when you start to race, or to try extending your limits, it can be frustrating if you don't know anything about training. Where do you go when you're in "excellent" condition and it's time to graduate from Kenneth Cooper's fitness program or whatever other schedule you've used to get into shape?

A few more basic principles are helpful at this stage. What you want to develop is what coach Arthur Lydiard calls "stamina" — the combination of speed and endurance. In training, you don't want to combine these two elements or you'll wear yourself out instead of building up reserves. Save the hard, fast runs for races. You can train almost 100% aerobically and still race well.

Most training programs nowadays (see Chapters 4-5) are eclectic combinations of long, steady runs, varied-pace runs, "intervals" and "speedwork" on the track and hill workouts. It is important to understand the purpose of each kind of running. Then you can design your own program, tailored to your own needs.

Endurance is built by long runs — pure mileage. Extending the daily runs helps, but the mainstay of endurance is the weekly "long jog" of roughly twice the average daily distance. Go as slowly as you like on these runs. Speed is irrelevant and can be wearing. The pace is generally even slower than the daily aerobic runs.

Endurance is the key to distance running. Lydiard points out that anyone can run a fast quarter-mile once. But putting four such fast quarters together for a record mile is a matter of endurance. So mileage and long runs are the base you must develop before adding any of the other training elements.

Speed. This is tougher to develop. Some people are born with good basic speed. They can move their legs fast for 100 or 220 yards — even when totally untrained. The rest of us have to work at it.

This speed shouldn't be confused with maximal aerobic pace — the speed you can go in a long race, the limit of what you can sustain for the distance. Maximal aerobic pace improves with endurance training. All you need is a bit of practice at moving along faster than you do in training. A weekly fun-race is ample practice.

"Speed-work," in contrast, is unrelated to endurance training. It is aimed at developing a tolerance for anaerobic running, for the discomfort of building up an oxygen debt. It helps to know what it feels like to run into oxygen debt, and that you won't die, though you may feel like it. Short intervals, sprints up to 440 yards and most track workouts are designed to build up this tolerance and to increase mechanical efficiency when moving fast, just through practice.

Speed-work of this type really is unnecessary for the intermediate runner — unless you have the ambition to run a fast mile or even a 440. Then it's essential. So if you enjoy track meets or want to participate in the expanding Masters track and field program, for instance, go ahead and try one or two interval workouts a week — *added to* your aerobic base.

But if you are happy as a road runner and don't care to race distances of a mile or less, you can ignore speed-work. The longer races themselves will be ample training for the faster pace used in racing. Even this "fast" running shouldn't exceed 5-10% of your total mileage or you'll be courting injury.

Strength. The third element in successful racing is the most limited in women, who are on the average 23% muscle vs. 40% for the average male. But even the 23% you have can be trained to become stronger.

Hill workouts are designed to build strength. This is where most men will outrun you most easily. Running up hills hard is painful and your thighs as well as your lungs will feel it. But if you run hills regularly, your body will, as always, adapt.

Try running in the mountains of Colorado some summer, at high altitude. There's an annual full-length marathon up and down Pike's Peak — from 7000 feet up to 14,000 and back down. Most "runners" walk the bulk of the uphill because the air is thin and the slope is steep. But after Pike's Peak, all the local hills look flat by comparison and you'll breeze up them — a miracle of adaptation.

Avoid using weight machines to build strength for running. I'm convinced that the best training for running hills is running hills. I'm biased, having hurt myself a couple of times on weight machines. But there's no exercise in a gym that can exactly duplicate the motions and the muscular stresses needed for running uphill.

YOUR OWN SCHEDULE

You'll find a lot of runners who are training on someone else's program. The theory behind this is that if it works for one person who is winning all the local races, it'll be right for others. This is wrong. Each person is different, and I'd be a wreck if I tried to follow, for example, the 100-mile-a-week schedule of marathon record holder Jacki Hansen. In fact, a single one of her interval workouts would probably do me in.

Conversely, I'm sure I wouldn't match the outstanding performances of marathoner Gayle Barron on her relatively light training. Gayle was third at Boston in 1975, running 2:54, yet she seldom trains more than 60 miles a week and hates all speed work, so simply doesn't do it.

Here are a couple of *sample* schedules for the intermediate level — one for 30 miles a week, one for 40. Notice the hard-easy pattern which is very helpful both in making progress and in recovering from the training stress. The sample weeks start on Sunday and end Saturday, but you can vary this if you like. (* = race)

Total	Sun.	Mon.	Tue.	Wed.	Thu.	Fri.	Sat.
30 miles	8	2	5	7	3	0	5*
40 miles	12	3	5	10	5	0	5*

These schedules allow for one rest day a week, one long run and one race — which shouldn't be all-out if it exceeds 10% of the weekly mileage, as in these examples. Use it as practice "pace-work." All the other daily runs are at comfortable, talking pace — whatever that is for you.

The rest day is important to give the body a chance to repair itself, if necessary. You may have subtle little aches or other symptoms of overstress that you wouldn't notice, but which can add up over the weeks to cause trouble. Scheduling this complete break before a race guarantees you'll be fresh and energetic for that run.

If you don't race weekly, try to run faster than usual in that day's workout or go to the track and try several shorter, faster runs — like quarter- or half-miles — to get the feeling of moving at race pace.

RATE OF PROGRESS

Most women won't become road racing stars overnight. Many of the changes in your body that result from training are very slow in coming. They are measured in months and years rather than weeks. You should continue to improve *automatically* for several years on a program of regular; steady runs. You needn't add speed-work, hills, double workouts or esoteric training methods to see progress.

If, after a couple of years, you find yourself on a definite plateau of performance, you can experiment — adding a little speed work, for instance, or increasing your mileage to more demanding levels. Whenever you make a change like this, the results won't be apparent for at least a month and probably not for six weeks or more. In fact, this year's championship performances often reflect the training of the previous year — or two or three years.

My own timetable of running may be instructive, though most women nowadays can progress much more rapidly than I did. I started at age 30, knew nothing about running or training, was not athletic, and suffered countless injuries requiring layoffs in the early months (and years). But here's roughly how I progressed — with fits and starts.

Year One (1971). Worked up from one mile twice a week to three miles (average) five times a week. When not injured, ran 15-20 miles a week, with two rest days (weekends). Longest run was seven miles (twice). Ran in two races, the Bay to Breakers (7.8 miles) and a hilly seven-miler. Walked almost half of each race, having started too fast.

Year Two (1972). Got my first stress fracture. Mileage improved to 30 per week in 5-6 days of running. Went to a summer running camp and learned about training. Raced up Pike's Peak (13 miles) but not down. Longest daily run was seven miles. Joined the Dolphin-South End club and entered 17 races.

Year Three (1973). Increased mileage again, up to 40 a week. Still resting one day in seven. Thirty-five races, including two marathons (both 3:17). Began doing weekly 20-mile training runs, at least in the last six weeks before marathons. Still injured intermittently.

Year Four (1974). Average weekly mileage now 60 — when not injured. Five marathons, including 2:58 in Germany (with the US National Team). Added a few hill workouts and interval sessions to the program (perhaps a total of 10 for the year).

Year Five (1975). Similar to 1974. Three thousand miles, 36 races, one pulled muscle, numerous aches, four marathons.

Noteworthy points: (1) I had a backlog of two years of running and more than 30 races (5-15 miles) before trying a marathon. (2) Whenever I increased my mileage in a fit of enthusiasm or ambition, I got injured. But even my weak protoplasm eventually adjusted to the higher stress load. (3) I was quite successful in racing without any special speed work or super-high mileage.

I make these points because I consider myself very ordinary — certainly not especially talented. And if I could progress on that kind of low-key training, it *has* to be the regularity that is crucial — not any special secrets. Many women now build up much faster and can tackle high mileage (say, 80 miles a week) or a marathon within a year of starting. They must have stronger bodies than I. In any case, I feel it's very important to have plenty of experience racing at shorter distances before tackling the long races, or you may have such a painful experience that you'll want to forget all about running.

four

Racers

Training nowadays tends to be highly individualistic and eclectic, a bit taken from Mihaly Igloi's fast interval method, a "base" of long running — fast or slow, according to preference — a dash of hill work here and cross-country there. The combinations are endless and the books written about different methods seem innumerable.

But it was not always so. Until the 1960s, fashions in training were almost as tyrannical as fashions in the clothing industry. Each new outstanding runner would be studied, his training methods analyzed and his program copied for the "benefit" of countless schoolboys, college students and national teams.

Naturally, since no individual's training program is ideal for everyone else, many of these unfortunate imitators ended up injured or bored. Only a few flourished and became champions themselves. Almost without exception, runners retired when they graduated from college and were no longer in a coached program. The only distance runners at the time were men, but the same general patterns held true for the women runners who were limited to sprints.

A BRIEF HISTORY OF METHODS

At the turn of the century, an era when the Boston Marathon (short course) was won in times around 2:40, the Olympic Marathon in about 3:00, training was haphazard. Distance runners took many long walks but ran few miles. Milers in the US right up through the '30s favored wind sprints, a few fast 440s and starting practice as preparation for their races.

The greatest distance runner of the '20s, and perhaps of the century, was Paavo Nurmi of Finland. His training was extensive by the standards of his time. For one thing, he ran daily in addition to frequent long walks. The runs would be 6-10 miles through the woods, supplemented by workouts of 5-6 fast quarter-miles several times a week.

With this background, incredibly low mileage by today's standards, Nurmi dominated the running world. Most people who imitated his program, or what they thought was his program, emphasized the fast short runs rather than the daily jogs in the woods. Their concept was that you had to train fast in order to race fast.

In the '30s, the Swedes introduced a popular training method called "fartlek," which can be translated as "speed play." Fartlek involves varying tempo runs, preferably through the woods and fields so that the terrain is constantly changing and imposes changes of effort and pace. Most of the running is brisk, and in its original form the run was interrupted periodically by "exercise breaks" involving vigorous calisthenics.

The Swedish runners, epitomized by Gunder Haegg, were quite successful and were renowned for their smooth, floating style, though how they developed this floating quality while running on trails through the woods, I don't know. Perhaps the Swedish trails have fewer logs, rocks and roots to jump than American woods.

The next revolutionary individual was Emil Zatopek of Czechoslovakia, who appeared totally unheralded in the 1948 Olympics and astounded the public by winning the gold medal in the 10,000 meters and the silver in the 5000. In 1952, he returned to the Olympics and won three gold medals in the 10,000, 5000 and marathon. His wife did her part by winning a gold medal in the javelin.

Naturally, everyone clamored to learn Zatopek's training secrets. His unorthodox and individualistic methods were

*Californians Karen Scannell and Lorraine Rorke taking the
big step up to their first marathon.*

somewhat misunderstood and led to some unfortunate future
training developments in both the US and Europe.

Zatopek popularized "interval training." That is, instead of
using steady runs or a few sharp sprints like Nurmi, he primarily
used numerous runs over certain intervals like 400 meters at one
pace, interspersed with shorter recovery jogs at slower pace.

Zatopek would do prodigious numbers of such repeats in his daily training, as many as 60-80 x 400 meters or a total of 20-30 miles. As Dr. Ernst van Aaken points out, the individual 400-meter runs were relatively slow, with only occasional faster runs. Thus, these workouts were actually a form of endurance training.

But "interval work" has come to mean almost the opposite — a set of *fast* repeats, often with very short recovery periods. This kind of training has its uses, of course, but cannot possibly be equivalent in *quantity* to Zatopek's training. Zatopek, an incredibly tough runner, would not have attempted 80 x 400 meters at the speeds employed by his misguided imitators. Some marathoners in Europe were even trained on such programs as 100 x 200 meters at sprint speed. Given the limits of the human organism, it is not surprising that many runners broke down on these programs and few improved.

Heavy doses of interval runs were used most successfully by Igloi, a Hungarian coach in the mid-1950s. One of his pupils, Laszlo Tabori, the world's third sub-4:00 miler, moved to the US after the 1956 Olympics and became a successful coach himself. Jacki Hansen and Miki Gorman, who both have held the women's world record in the marathon, train with Tabori and do intervals 2-3 times per week.

The Igloi-Tabori interval workouts differ in several respects from those of Zatopek. The runs are much faster than those favored by Zatopek, usually racing speed or faster, and there are fewer repeats. The programs are extremely varied and no two days or workouts will be identical. Each runner is given his or her own assignment. The emphasis is definitely on speed and anaerobic runs (those that build up an oxygen debt and have you gasping for breath at the end) rather than on endurance.

In practice, runners like Hansen and Gorman rely on aerobic long runs and high mileage to develop their endurance, and use the interval workouts to build up their speed and racing ability.

These modern "mixed" running programs are influenced

most strongly by the most recent guru of running, Arthur
Lydiard of New Zealand. Like Igloi, Lydiard is an inspired
coach whose methods achieved prominence through the success
of his pupils — most notably Peter Snell and Murray Halberg,
who both won gold medals in the 1960 Olympics, while a third
pupil, Barry Magee, took the bronze in the marathon.

Lydiard, like Dr. van Aaken in Germany, emphasized the
importance of long daily runs and high total mileage even for
runners at distance of 800 and 1500 meters (Snell's gold medal
events in 1964). Lydiard introduced the "base" of 100 miles
per week, which has since been adopted by countless runners —
from Olympic athletes through high school runners. One
hundred miles a week, once regarded as so physically demanding as to be almost impossible, is now almost routine.

Other parts of Lydiard's teachings have been less popular,
notably his emphasis on rather grueling hill workouts. Equally
important concepts derived from Lydiard are "peaking" and the
related "sharpening." Lydiard states that one can time the
training program so as to produce one's best performance on a
particular day (once a year in practice). This is done by adding
hill workouts, and later varied interval, pace and speed
workouts, to the solid "base" of endurance. Lydiard and
Oregon's famous coach, Bill Bowerman, exchanged ideas frequently and both favor the hard/easy pattern of training.

Today's runners, then, have a wealth of diverse training
methods to draw upon, according to their own inclination.
Since the mid-1960s, as road racing has developed, many have
continued to run beyond the college years, and are self-coached.
They use whatever method helps them to improve without
becoming injured or ill.

If intervals cause fast progress but result in frequent
muscle pulls or illnesses, intervals can be dropped in favor of
LSD (long, slow distance). Conversely, if one is tired of
continual long runs, or is on a plateau of achievement, the
program can be spiced up with a few hard hills or weekly
interval workouts. Fartlek is a very popular method of
combining speed with scenic runs.

Today's eclectic, self-coached runner can enjoy running and playing with different methods in a way that was impossible for the "programmed" runner of the '50s or early '60s. And women, who have escaped the rigid, one-track coaching programs of the schools, and who run primarily for enjoyment, have the freest choice of all.

HISTORY OF WOMEN'S LONG DISTANCE RUNNING

One of the great ironies of sport is that women, considered to be the "weaker sex," have been limited to sprint events — 100-yard dashes and so forth — until very recently. And the younger (hence, the "weaker") the girls, the shorter the distance permitted so that grade school girls were confined to the 40-yard stretches. The fact that more explosive power, and hence more muscle, is required for sprints than for long distances was simply overlooked.

Orthodox, and uninformed, medical opinion tried to protect women from overtaxing themselves and perhaps killing themselves by attempting the half-mile. The marathon was considered a physical impossibility for females. The medical and sports establishment reacted in disbelief when a 15-year-old Canadian girl, Maureen Wilton, was reported to have run a marathon in 1967. (It was true, however, and her time, 3:15:22, was the unofficial women's world record.)

Early experience with "long distances" for women appeared to support these fears, most dramatically during the 1928 Olympic Games, when an 800-meter race for women was introduced. The women who entered this event were all sprinters — 100- and 200-meter runners — and like all sprinters of that era, had virtually no training. Sprints do not require high aerobic capacity, but the 800-meter race is different, even though no one realized it. The women sprinters in 1928 dashed out at close to their best 200-meter pace and then tried to hang on. The result was a disaster. Most of the competitors collapsed or finished the race in such pain and distress that officials were shocked and horrified — as well as convinced, more than ever, that women are physiologically unsuited for distance running.

The 800 meters for women was banned from the Olympics until 1964, and even in 1976 the longest Olympic run for women was 1500 meters (less than a mile).

The 800-meter competition was reintroduced in Europe in the 1950s, largely because of continued pressure from Dr. Ernst van Aaken, a leading advocate of distance running for everyone, young and old, men and women. Dr. van Aaken pointed out that women are built for endurance rather than explosive power and *if properly trained*, should excel at long distances.

The establishment was still skeptical, nonetheless, and insisted on proper precautions when the 800-meter race was reintroduced. Ambulances were stationed at the finish line — motors running, lights flashing, all revved up to take the casualties to the nearest hospital. To the surprise of all but Dr. van Aaken, there were no casualties.

Liane Winter, winner of the Boston Marathon in 1975 and of the first International Women's Marathon in Waldniel, Germany, in 1974, recalls those days well.

"We were lucky to be allowed to run 1000 meters over grass in the cross-country events," she said.

Winter was good enough to belong to the team that won the German national cross-country championship in that era, but the real talent was only apparent at distances 42 times as long. She didn't get a chance to utilize this talent until marathoning for women became respectable after 1972.

"Permission" for women to run the marathon was granted by the AAU in a blanket capitulation in 1972. All distances for women runners, formerly limited to a mile on the track (slightly farther in cross-country) were okayed.

At the time of this writing, only the marathon and 10-kilometer runs are recognized as national championships. But women are now welcome officially in such competitions as the Boston Marathon and the San Francisco Bay-to-Breakers race (the largest race in the US with more than 6000 participants).

Official endorsement of women's right to run long distances followed many years of silent rebellion and covert participation by the female pioneers of road running, such women as Kathrine Switzer of New York and Elaine Pedersen of San Francisco. Back in the late '60s, both shared the dubious honor of being officially ejected from local races. As more and more women joined the pioneers, officials tended to look the other way and finally the AAU figuratively threw up its hands in despair and said, in effect, "They're running whether we like it or not. We might as well sanction the *fait accompli.*"

Nowadays, the struggle is not to be allowed to run, but more for such minor matters as having women listed as a separate division in the race results, with proportionate awards, and in age groups comparable to those of men. The Women's Masters movement (for women runners over 40 years of age) is gaining strength and increasing recognition as a separate division.

The worst battles are over for the US. In Europe, however, many women are still barred from "official" road runs (most notably in France and Belgium) and have reacted by flocking to the anti-establishment "Spiridon" (Road Runners Club), which has no age or sex restrictions.

The burgeoning participation of women in long-distance running has resulted in phenomenally fast progression of records. For example, the men's marathon world record stood at 2:08:33.6 for more than seven years (Derek Clayton of Australia set it in 1969 by breaking his own 1967 record of 2:09:36.4).

Now look at the women's record progression:

1967	3:15:22	Maureen Wilton (Canada)
1967	3:07:26	Anni Pede-Erdkamp (W. Ger.)
1970	3:02:53	Caroline Walker (US)
1971	3:01:42	Beth Bonner (US)
1971	3:00:35	Sara Berman (US)
1971	2:55:22	Beth Bonner (US)
1971	2:49:40	Cheryl Bridges (US)
1973	2:46:36	Miki Gorman (US)
1974	2:46:24	Chantal Langlace (Fr.)

1974	2:43:54	Jacqueline Hansen (US)
1975	2:42:24	Liane Winters (W. Ger.)
1975	2:40:15	Christa Vahlensieck (W. Ger.)
1975	2:38:19	Jacqueline Hansen (US)

It is interesting to note than the three German record holders listed are all proteges of Dr. van Aaken, the foremost European advocate of distance running for women.

The remarkable improvement in recent years reflects the fact that until 1971 only a scattered handful of women were running long. As thousands of women begin testing their talents in this newly opened field, new abilities and speed become apparent. Not only the world leaders are faster but also the masses are faster. Until 1971, three hours was the "impossible barrier" for women in the marathon. In 1975 alone, 27 women ran under that magic mark and 2:30 has become the new "impossible barrier."

MARATHONING

Marathon running seems like such an improbable activity that one wonders at its popularity. The distance, 26 miles 385 yards, seems illogical as well as excessive, especially when you're running the last six miles. No other kind of race finds the majority of the participants wondering somewhere along the way just what the hell they are doing.

Once, before the Boston Marathon, some reporters from a local paper asked me the usual question, "Why are you entering such a grueling event?"

It's always described as "grueling," but "nonsensical" would be more to the point. I didn't give Sir Edmund Hilary's classic answer, "Because it's there," but a much less noble reason, "For fun, I suppose." Around the 23-mile mark, I recalled that statement with a shudder of disbelief and realized I was getting my just desserts.

Why, then, run a marathon? I suppose in part it's a flocking instinct. Most road runners aim at working up to a marathon and one tends to go along with the crowd. Convenience is another criterion since there are more than 150 marathons in the US every year, one in every neighborhood, it seems, whereas equally prestigious and significant shorter races are rare.

The marathon, being the first official road race (introduced in the 1896 Olympics and the following year at Boston), has the advantage of long tradition. Nowadays, most courses are certified (the distance must be accurate, making time standards comparable). And most importantly, marathons *are* fun, at least when you're not in the last fatiguing stages.

I have several special reasons for running marathons, reasons which may not apply to all runners. I like to excel and I don't have much leg speed or talent, only persistence. So the longer distance is definitely to my advantage since one can train endurance even if one can't improve on basic speed. I was fortunate enough to make the National AAU Marathon team in 1974 and 1976, whereas at shorter distances I'm left in the dust by the fleet of young women who train on a steady diet of intervals. In the 1975 AAU Cross-Country Championship, I finished 61st, somewhere in the middle of the pack, on the three-mile course. I returned to the marathon with a sigh of relief two weeks later.

This brings up another reason why I like marathons as compared to the three-mile or, worse yet, the mile. Marathons are relatively comfortable. I was in agony every step of the cross-country run. A near-maximal effort was required, my lungs ached, my legs felt like lead. You can't sustain this kind of effort for 26 miles, obviously.

The early miles — in fact, the first 20 or so — of the marathon are very pleasant. You can float along smoothly at your fastest *aerobic* pace (you must stay aerobic), moving comfortably, talking if you like. Only when leg fatigue sets in, followed by total body fatigue in the last miles, does the experience become distinctly painful.

But there are all kinds of pain, and personally I prefer the fatigue-type pain of the late marathon to the burning throat and heavy legs of the mile or three-mile. It's all a matter of what you're accustomed to. A 440-yard runner considers the cross-country distance a supreme test of endurance. To me, it's a sprint.

Finally, I keep returning to the marathon because of its unpredictable nature. You never know how its going to turn out until you've crossed the finish line. You could be sailing along, having a great day and cramp up completely in the last miles or yards. Or you can feel sluggish and heavy in the first 10-15 miles, then gain energy and speed as you progress. The challenge is always there, first to finish, later to improve your personal record. If all has gone perfectly and you've accomplished your goal, you immediately set another harder goal. If one of the vagaries of the marathon has stopped you today, there's always another chance ahead.

No other race possesses this quality of uncertainty and challenge. In races of 3-20 miles, you can pretty well predict how you'll do, on the basis of training, speed and performance in other races. This is not so with the marathon. It can always surprise you.

You go into the race with fingers crossed and breathing prayers to propitiate the spirit of the marathon. Superstition plays an important role. Marathoners all have their own little rituals, related to diet, training (especially the week before), clothes and shoes. There is no rational basis for these little rituals, generally. They are actually designed to placate the gods. Lesser races, which reflect more accurately the runner's condition and training, seldom elicit such illogical behavior.

MARATHON TRAINING AND RACING

It isn't hard to run a marathon. Virtually anyone can do it on a modicum of training. But if you want to finish in good condition and run a second and further marathons, proper training is vital.

A true beginner should plan on at least a year of running, preferably two or more, before tackling the marathon distance. During these years, she should aim for consistency and gradually increased mileage. In order to finish in, say, four hours or less, one should aim for roughly 40 miles per week

Age is no more a handicap for women than men. Ruth Anderson (F33), shown here in the 1976 Boston Marathon, ran 3:05 at the age of 46.

Jeff Johnson

for at least two months before the race, with five or more long weekend runs of 20 miles. The long runs are crucial.

Some runners suggest using a time schedule rather than mileage as your guide. Work up to running an hour per day (average) with a 2-3-hour "long run" once a week. Combine this schedule with a good dose of racing at shorter distances and you'll be in good shape for your first marathon.

Nowhere is proper pacing more important than in the marathon. Don't go into this race thinking, "Well, I'm inevitably going to slow down as I get tired, so I'd better start out fast." This doesn't work. Instead, pick a pace you can run comfortably — it may seem slow — and stick with this for the whole 26.2 miles. If you've chosen the correct pace, you won't slow down. In fact, you may even accelerate at the end, as did Jacki Hansen in her world-record marathon in 1975. Jacki's first mile, in 6:07, was actually her slowest of the race. She passed 10 miles in 60:15, 20 miles in 2:01, then was so excited she accelerated slightly to exactly 6:00 mile pace from there to the finish. This is a model of exact pacing.

On a more modest scale, say you want to qualify for the Boston Marathon by running 3:30 or better. If you run even eight-minute miles, you'll finish in 3:29:45, perhaps shaving it a bit too close for comfort. So, if you really want to run Boston, perhaps you should start off at 7:50 pace, giving a 3:25:23, if maintained, and allowing for slight miscalculations of your capacity.

You can find complete "5-50 mile pacing charts" in the appendix and write down your intermediate time goals ("splits") on your arm before the race. I find this useful because after I've been running hard for 10 miles or more, I find myself unable to calculate very well or even to count accurately. I don't know if this arithmetical breakdown reflects low blood sugar, lack of oxygen to the brain or simply concentration on running, but it's a common phenomenon.

To return to our first-time marathoner aiming for Boston, she'll find (or can calculate) that 7:50 pace equals 39:10 for five miles, 1:18:20 for 10 miles and so on. If the race directors are kind enough to call out accurate splits at one, three and five miles, the runner can adjust her pace accordingly. Don't worry if the 7:50 (or whatever) pace seems slow to you. If it's the right pace, you'll be able to maintain it and eventually will pass many of those hot-shots who charge out past you at the start, impatient with your easy tempo.

How do you select the proper pace? Not just out of the blue. In your *best* marathon, you can aim eventually for a pace approximately one minute per mile slower than your fastest mile pace. If you can run a six-minute mile, you should ultimately be capable of a marathon around 3:03 (seven-minute pace). If you're a five-minute miler and work on endurance, you someday should be able to duplicate Jacki Hansen's feat of running 26.2 miles at six-minute pace. And if you can barely average seven-minute miles for short (3-4-mile) races, 3:30 should be your ultimate marathon goal.

In your first marathon, you should run slower than this ultimate "goal pace." Try adding on 30 seconds per mile, to compensate for your lack of experience at the distance. Or else take your best average for a 10-mile race and pace yourself a full minute per mile slower in your first marathon. Your body will thank you for your consideration and you'll end up tired but not wiped out or discouraged.

I have observed that most older women who progress from jogging and fun-runs to the marathon pace themselves wisely and approach their real potential for the distance. Younger girls, particularly those accustomed to the faster pace of track races, almost invariably go out too fast in the marathon (and other long races). They'll often start out 30 seconds per mile slower than their best mile, and will be fooled because this seems so easy for the first five or 10 miles. In the later stages of the marathon, they slow painfully and sometimes are on the verge of collapse.

It is unwise, until you are an experienced marathoner, to run according to how you feel rather than according to a preset schedule. You may on occasion have to run without knowing your pace, if no splits (or inaccurate ones) are given. But try, for your first race, to choose a race which has accurate splits and make good use of them.

If you have no idea what 8:00 pace or 7:50 or 6:50 feels like, and if you usually just run with the pack, it would be helpful to groove in on your desired pace the week before the race. All you need is a track (or measured mile) and a stopwatch. Run repeat miles, with your eye on the second hand, aiming for precisely the right pace. Notice how fast your legs are moving, be aware of your breathing and so forth. You should feel very comfortable and relaxed. Remember, you'll be doing this for more than 26 miles. Get to know what your pace feels like ahead of time, and don't be lured into a faster pace by the excitement or the pack.

In any long run, and especially a long race, you'll lose huge amounts of fluid. Women are probably more susceptible to fluid loss than men, because of women's higher fat content. Fat contains less water than muscle does and the water lost in sweat is more apt to diminish the blood volume in women than men whose 40% muscle (and corresponding large glycogen stores) will supply water for some time.

Moral: be sure to drink plenty of fluids as you run – even before you experience thirst. Take at least a few swallows at each aid station. If the day is warm, you'll need much more. Pour some on your head, too (but don't get your shoes wet or you'll have blisters).

Personally, I like either water or ERG (a dilute salt and sugar solution) on the run. Some marathoners prefer diluted fruit juices or Coke, which make me sick. You'll have to find your own brew. Gatorade, even diluted, upsets my stomach when I'm racing and generally I steer clear of any drinks containing magnesium. Runners have enough trouble with diarrhea without adding to their woes by ingesting dilute milk of magnesia. You can replace your lost salts – sodium, potassium and magnesium – after the run. Only fluid replacement is vital during the race.

Whichever brew you choose, try it out on your weekend long runs so you'll know in advance what concoction you can tolerate and how much. Some of my beer-guzzling marathon friends have been known to stash six-packs discretely along the route of their long runs or races. They claim this gives a pause that truly refreshes, but then they generally run marathons for fun and to finish, not for a good time.

Alcohol, even diluted with helpful fluid and vitamins as in beer, *does* interfere with neuromuscular functioning and is not recommended for the runner pushing to his (or her) maximal capacity. Better, for most of us, to stash a jar of water or ERG along the way. Take Coke, if you insist on being decadent, but defizz it first by letting it stand overnight.

But, just to make the point that people are all different, I know one man who runs marathons *fast* on fizzy Coke. He swears the constant belching resulting from this bubbly brew relaxes him and enhances his racing.

five

Schedules

I should make it clear at the outset that these schedules, and the principles behind them, are not original with me. My own training and my thoughts about it are derived from the ideas of Ron Daws, a member of the 1968 Olympic team, who has more than 20 years of running experience to draw on. Daws' training, in turn, is largely derived from Arthur Lydiard, with modifications to meet Ron's own needs and special conditions (like the Minnesota winters).

So if you want more details or would prefer the original to the modified form, check the books of Daws and Lydiard listed in the appendix. The major changes I've made for myself and other women are to reduce the recommended mileage by about one-third and to keep the training more or less the same all year rather than aiming to peak for a specific race or season.

The basis of advanced training is to build a solid foundation of endurance running. Upon this foundation of relatively high but easy-paced mileage, one can then add increasing amounts of hill work for strength and races or interval work for speed.

Thus, to build a base, one starts with an intermediate schedule (page 31) based on 30-40 miles per week and gradually increases the load until the mileage is doubled, with two training sessions being run on Tuesday, Wednesday and Thursday. For example:

Total	Sun	Mon	Tue	Wed	Thu	Fri	Sat
80 miles	20	7	3/12	5/5	3/12	3	10

If you are employed, the easiest way to get in the base mileage is by running to work and back:

Total	Sun	Mon	Tue	Wed	Thu	Fri	Sat
80 miles	20	5/5	5/5	5/5	5/5	5/5	10

If you live more than five miles from work, you can always drive part of the way and leave your car. You'll save on parking fees.

The first schedule, of course, has several advantages over the second. You can vary the route and thus avoid boredom, the hard/easy pattern allows the body to recover better and Friday becomes a good "rest day." But schedule two is definitely more convenient and you don't have to check your schedule to remember what the day's workout is.

The 80-mile total is arbitrary. If you'd prefer 60 or 100, simply add or subtract miles as needed.

Several principles are important in this phase of endurance build-up. The long run one day a week should be firmly scheduled or you'll find excuses to avoid it. This run, more than anything, keeps your legs and metabolism adjusted to long-distance running. Don't cut it. It doesn't matter how slow you go on the long run — it's for *endurance*, not speed. The same applies to the daily run during this phase of training. Don't worry about pace. Just get in the miles.

You'll notice the double workouts 3-5 days per week. These should be introduced one at a time if possible, so as not to tire yourself. This is the easiest way to increase mileage drastically without realizing how much more you're doing. The body recovers sufficiently in the 6-12-hour interval between sessions to be fooled into thinking it's the first run of the day.

I find I often feel lousy during the easy morning run, but much better — warmed up, perhaps — later in the day. In fact, I ran my best five-mile race in the evening after a morning seven-mile jog. The aim of the morning run is to add mileage and get you loosened up, not to add another hard workout. Take it easy.

Finally, try to stick to a hard/easy pattern whenever possible. You can juggle the week around however you like — putting the long run on Wednesday, for example — but don't disrupt the pattern which is designed to develop a regular rhythm of work and recovery in the body.

Arthur Lydiard suggests six weeks to six months for this build-up, depending on your initial condition. I'd recommend a minimum of two months. It takes time for your body to adapt and to see the results of increased mileage or other variations in training.

You can do the build-up yearly, as in Lydiard's original program, or twice a year, or just once in your running career. It depends on how hard you push yourself at other times. The harder and faster you race after the build-up, the more your body will need the recovery months of long, but easy, mileage.

After this build-up you will feel as strong as an ox. You may also feel (and be) as slow and lumbering as an ox. You may be able to run for miles and miles, but at the same old plodding pace. It is comforting to realize that once you have the endurance base, speed can be added on extremely quickly. All you need is a little practice and time. You'll see the results in 4-6 weeks.

There are numerous ways of practicing speed. Dr. Ernst van Aaken advocates a fast, short run, maybe a half-mile, at the end of each daily long jog. Tom Osler, in *The Conditioning of Distance Runners*, suggests inserting several half-mile "pick-ups" plus a few 50-yard sprints for leg speed, into the daily run, several times a week.

In my first few years of running, the *only* speed work I did was racing, about every 1-2 weeks, usually 5-10 miles. You may prefer to run 1-2 fartlek workouts through the woods. These are fun if you go with a friend and alternate choosing the distance and speed of the "pick-up" sections.

Lydiard follows his endurance build-up with 4-6 weeks of special hill workouts to be described later, and then 3-4 weeks of "sharpening" on the track. This kind of program aims at peak performance after the sharpening weeks. If Lydiard's pupils appear to be "peaking" too soon, he'll slow down their sharpening deliberately to keep the original schedule.

Finally, you can use the classic interval training on a track. Once or twice a week is enough. These workouts appeal especially to those who want to know exactly how hard they are pushing themselves, by knowing accurate distances and times. They also enable you to measure improvement from week to week and as such are extremely encouraging, since improvement in speed comes amazingly fast after endurance is established.

The aim of all forms of speed work is the same: to prepare you for running at a racing pace by getting you used to the feeling of fast running. You'll get out of breath, your legs will feel heavy and you'll definitely feel awkward at first. But after a few sessions, the motions will have been learned, the pace will seem easier and you'll no longer be afraid of dying as you push to the point of breathlessness.

The greatest block may be mental. You feel in agony when you run a fast mile, and it takes several tries before you realize you can keep going and survive. I was greatly helped by a remark by Bobbi Moore, the wife of marathoner Kenny Moore, who was also suffering in her attempts to run a sub-6:00 mile.

"Kenny said to me, 'It's *supposed* to hurt. Don't worry,' " she said.

Keep that in mind and it will ease the transition from road running to speed work. The speed work will train your anaerobic capacity and that *does* hurt. It's *supposed* to. Soon you'll be better able to tolerate the oxygen debt and you can either speed up (and keep hurting) or run the same pace without pain, having, as always, adapted.

If you choose to take your dose of speed once or twice a week, rather than daily, here's a sample schedule (very similar to my own):

Total	Sun	Mon	Tue	Wed	Thu	Fri	Sat
70 miles	20	5	3/7 (I)	5/5	3/8 (I)	7	Race or 7 hilly

Tuesday and Thursday are the speed work days, plus

Saturday if there's a race. But the total of 15 miles marked "I" (for interval) is not all fast. It includes warmup, cooldown and recovery jogs. The experience of many different runners and trainers has shown that your speed work shouldn't exceed 10% of your total mileage, on the average — in the above schedule, only seven miles. A little bit — as little as 5%, according to van Aaken — goes a long way. Fifteen percent consistently could be excessive and might ultimately result in injury or overtraining.

The mileage in my example has been reduced slightly from the endurance phase. This is done deliberately to compensate for the increased stress of the speed sessions.

I should add here, for the sake of any high school or college runners reading this book, that races are the equivalent of a speed workout. Thus, if you're racing twice a week, you should use the other days for easy recovery runs, *not* for hard interval training. Let's hope you have a coach who understands the principles. If you race the half-mile and up, you could benefit also from one brief session of short intervals, such as 5 x 220 fast or 10 x 100 fast. These will help your speed, which is not really practiced in races. Your "long run" during track racing season can be one hour, two hours during cross-country, but you'll have to do the bulk of your training before the season starts and generally just rest up between frequent races in season.

LYDIARD HILL WORKOUTS

For the purists or masochists or both among you, who would like to adhere strictly to Arthur Lydiard's program, I'll describe the hill workouts. For me, they are torture, but then I've run my best marathons off of this kind of training, so perhaps it works.

The Lydiard program calls for 4-6 weeks of these sessions, three times per week. Many successful marathoners, however, cut this to twice, or even once, per week. Hill work should be done after the initial endurance phase, when you're strong and able to take the added stress. Otherwise it will wreck your body.

The recommended workout consists of four cycles of the following. Find a hill about a half-mile long. Run up it hard, jog about a half-mile on top (4-5 minutes) to recover fully, run downhill *fast* — but as relaxed as possible. Jog a bit, then do repeat sprints at the (hopefully flat) bottom of the hill (3 x 220 or 6 x 50 yards with equal distance jogs recovery).

The hot-shot runners (male) actually do this grueling cycle four times in succession. Then they stagger home and collapse, no doubt. I have never managed more than two cycles and felt that was a solid workout. If you feel really strong, try three. If you manage four, hard up and fast down, no cheating, write me about it!

INTERVALS

Intervals are the opposite of steady, even-paced running and are generally aimed at developing speed for racing, rather than endurance or stamina. There are certain famous exceptions, most notably the "founder" of modern interval training, Emil Zatopek. Zatopek used to run so many intervals — 80 x 400 meters, for instance — that he developed phenomenal endurance. But he ran them relatively slowly. The faster the intervals, the more tiring they are and the fewer you should do.

The idea of the interval training is to vary your pace — usually running set distances at race pace or even faster, then jogging or walking to recover from the effort, then repeating the fast run and so on. The distance run at race pace, of course, is shorter than the actual distance to be raced in competition. Thus, an 880-yard runner could do repeat 220s at race pace in training. A marathoner would get the same effect with repeat two-mile or mile intervals.

It follows from the preceding section that since interval training is designed to develop racing speed, it should be introduced *after* a solid endurance base has been built up. It won't help you much in your first year of running and the faster pace could very easily injure your legs. Wait until you're developed enough to benefit from a little speed work.

As with all transitions in training, you should introduce

intervals gradually. After Lydiard-type endurance training, your *forte* will be stamina and distance. Early workouts, therefore, should exploit this strength by emphasizing many repetitions at fairly easy pace (but not as slow as your usual training run; you want to get the feel of moving faster). Later on, you cut down the number of repetitions and increase speed. Sounds simple, doesn't it? Keep these basic principles in mind and you won't get bogged down in the details that follow.

As always, you should adapt the examples to your own needs. If you want to race faster at 6-10 miles, you should concentrate on the longer intervals — 880 and up. If some of the local all-comers meets stimulate you to try to get a good mile time, do plenty of 220s and 440s. Above all, listen to your body, watch your response and find what you like. You may find you hate the track. If so, do fartlek or "pickups" on the road — the effect will be the same.

In case you're not familiar with tracks (I certainly wasn't), the usual high school or college track (outdoor) is a quarter-mile around (440 yards) in the innermost lane. If you use an outside lane, the distance is longer and you'll have to look for the 440 "stagger lines" in each lane to know where to start. A 220 obviously is halfway around and a 110 is one-quarter of the circumference — or, if you prefer, the distance between the goal posts on the football field minus 10 yards.

Traditionally, one runs counter-clockwise on the track, starting at the "pole" before the first curve. But don't feel bound by tradition. Start wherever you like. Run clockwise if you like. It's often easier on the knees to run half the intervals in each direction.

It's important to warm up thoroughly before any fast running, so that you don't pull or strain a muscle (including your heart!). Personally, I like the warmup enforced by Laszlo Tabori, one of the first sub-4:00 milers, and at present the coach of Jacki Hansen and Miki Gorman (as well as of numerous male distance runners).

Tabori's pupils jog 2-3 miles, or about 20 minutes, over grass, chatting as they go. Then they assemble for some stretching and loosening-up exercises. Finally, they run 15 times up and down the field between goal posts. These fast runs, called "shake-ups," start off at good striding pace and get faster in the later repeats. The recovery is exceedingly short — just the time to walk behind the goal posts. When the warmup is over, the runners already have had a solid speed workout on grass to pamper their feet. The interval session proper is followed by another 9-10 shake-ups to cool down. (At this point, without Tabori standing over you, you may prefer just to jog a mile on your own track!)

As for the interval session proper, there's an infinite variety of combinations, repeats and so forth that you can devise for your own benefit. Almost anything will help, providing it's faster than your usual training pace and that you recover adequately. Hal Higdon says he likes "three of anything"—all-out, with full stops for recovery (five minutes or whatever). I prefer to keep moving during my workouts (to get them over with) and usually do more repeats but not all-out.

Tabori never gives two runners the same workout or any one runner the identical workout twice. He keeps them guessing. This adds interest to the workout but only works if you have a coach to set up the daily schedule.

Here are a few sample workouts (courtesy of Ron Daws):

Early Season (relatively slow pace)
1. Classic: 15-20 x 440 or 5 x one mile (half distance recovery).
2. Ladder: 1 x 1320, 2 x 880, 2 x 660, 2 x 440, 2 x 220.
3. Time trial of 2-3 miles, plus striding (110s and 220s).

Late Season (sharpening, faster pace)
1. Classic: 10 x 220 or 10 x 440 (equal distance recovery).
2. Ladder: 5 x 110, 4 x 220, 3 x 440, 4 x 220, 5 x 110.
3. Two miles of alternate 50-yard sprints and 60-yard jogs.
4. Twenty to 40 x 110 sprints run in sets of 10, 30 seconds, walk rest.
5. Uphill sprints of about 100 yards jog down.

Don't forget to warm up and cool off with a jog in each of these workouts. You'll find they go faster if you break them up into "sets" of four, five and so on, with a longer recovery between sets than between the intervals.

RACING AND PACING

The only way to learn to race is by racing. The main thing you'll learn is how to pace yourself or how fast you can run for how long. The early races are liable to be disasters of pacing, as you'll have no idea what your capabilities are. The tendency is to go out too fast and die. This is the major pitfall for younger girls, in whom enthusiasm and familiarity with faster, shorter track runs, outweighs both caution and any advice from more experienced racers. Older women have a tremendous advantage in racing since they usually will be fresh and strong when the younger girls (and boys) who charged out madly are dropping like flies.

I can well remember my first race. It was the 7.8-mile Bay-to-Breakers run across San Francisco, which lures about 5000 participants each year. I had only been running about three months and had never gone more than three miles, but decided to join the happening when I learned you could walk as much as you liked. Knowing I was capable of running three miles, that's precisely what I did — ran as fast as I could, three miles, right to the foot of the one big hill in the race. Then I walked all the way up the hill. I jogged down, and alternately walked and jogged for the remainder of the race.

This is an example of very poor pacing. The running parts were fast but the walking parts more than compensated, and I was passed by hundreds of the plodders who kept up a steady pace. It took me another six months and four more races before I was able to run one the whole way.

Some well-trained but cautious women have the opposite problem. They start out at a pace comparable to their training jog, tentatively speed up after a few miles, wait to see if they're tired, speed up again, and so forth. They finish with plenty of strength left, but are way back in the pack. Obviously this method doesn't exploit one's full potential either, though it certainly is comfortable.

One of our outstanding local marathoners ran three or four times around 3:30, always starting out cautiously, like nine minutes per mile, and speeding up to 6:40 pace for the last six miles. When she finally had enough confidence to start at 6:50 pace and hold it she ran 2:58, or a 24-minute improvement over her "turtle-tactics" best.

The only way to learn is by experience. And you have to take it on faith (and other runners' experiences) that the most efficient way to race is to spread your strength evenly over the full length of the course. This is especially important in the marathon, but applies to all races from the mile up. Don't go out at a pace you know is too fast, in order to "compensate" for the slowdown you fear in the second half of the race. With uneven pacing, the slowdown will more than offset the minutes gained by fast early pacing.

It's wise to taper off in your training for the last few days or week before a big race. At that point, the training sessions are too close to the race to influence your condition for it (except adversely, by making you tired or sore). Rest is more important. So for those last days, just jog easily and comfortably to loosen up and you'll be fresh the day of the "big one."

HOT WEATHER RACING

Racing in the heat can be extremely dangerous. A few runners have died of heat stroke and many have collapsed from heat exhaustion. If you *must* race on a hot day, drink plenty of (cold) fluids during the race, pour some (preferably water to avoid stickiness) over your head and pace yourself slower than usual for that distance. Wear white clothes and a white hat to reflect the sun. Symptoms of heat exhaustion include fatigue, headache and dizziness — also chilling sensations and goose flesh, indicating your heat-regulation center has been fouled up. If you get these symptoms, stop or walk, preferably in the shade. The idea is to cool yourself while you still can. Running and even walking generates more heat.

The most common victims of heat are young boys, who often seem determined to run themselves into the ground no

matter what symptoms they're having. They don't want to be
"quitters," or to let down the school, the coach, and so on. You
need to have none of these hang-ups, so use common sense.
Also beware of any medication — dexedrine, ephedrine, asthma
or hay fever pills — which may stimulate you so much you
don't recognize the symptoms of exhaustion until it is too late.
Most people who collapse were drugged in some way so they
couldn't heed the body's warnings.

   Finally, if you know you'll be racing in the heat, you can
train for it by running in the heat for 2-3 weeks before the race.
If you have no local heat (as in foggy San Francisco), you can
get the same effect by wearing lots of sweat clothes. You must
feel uncomfortably hot to do effective heat training.

Part II

Aids and Advice

six

Shoes

Shoes are the single most important item of equipment. In fact, they're the only important part. You can wear old, scruffy blue jeans and a baggy sweatshirt, or even run in the nude if you prefer, but your feet must be well shod. The proper shoes will help prevent injuries, whether you're a beginning jogger or a world-class marathoner.

A lot of beginning runners feel embarrassed about going to a sports shop and buying a pair of flashy $25-30 running flats. "Oh, I'll just use my tennis shoes (Hush Puppies, loafers and so forth) till I see if I like running," they think.

But even if you use your brand new $35 Billie Jean King tennis specials, chances are you'll end up with sprained ankles or shin splints plus a deep dislike for running, remembering those heavy shoes or the injuries.

So spend the money now when the proper shoe will be most needed. Having made such a cash investment, you'll be less tempted to drop out during the initial, often painful phase of getting into basic condition.

What kind of shoes should you get? *Not* "track shoes," which are flimsy things with spikes for traction in dirt, but "road running flats." Flats are of two basic types — training and racing. Some models can be used for both. The difference is in weight, cushioning and support. For your daily runs, you want a sturdy pair of training shoes with a half-inch to an inch of cushioning under the foot to soften your impact on asphalt or cement.

The best shoes are usually of leather or lightweight nylon reinforced with leather. Good nylon models have a fitted leather heel cup, not just a thin strip, which prevents the foot from rolling and the ankle from twisting. Look for a shoe with the heel slightly higher than the toe, so as to reduce strain on the achilles tendon.

Beyond these points, just try on various models and find which fits you best and feels most comfortable. You'll be amazed at how good your feet feel in well-fitted running shoes. You'll never want to take them off.

Judy Ikenberry, the 1974 women's national marathon champion, wore her new, soft suede racing flats to a party under a long skirt. She gave an interview on German television and at the end of it was asked by one of the reporters to lift her skirt, revealing her practical footgear, to the delight of the German public.

It's difficult to designate a "best model" because the width of shoes and shape of the last varies from one brand to the next and even among different models from the same company. Allow at least a half-inch of toe room in any shoes.

The better models of training flats in the nylon category are Adidas (SL 72 and SL 76), Brooks (various models), New Balance (3:05 or 3:20), Nike (Cortez, Road Runner and Waffle Trainer), Puma (9190) and Tiger (Montreal 76). The top models of leather shoes include Adidas (Country), EB (Lydiard Road Runners and Universal), New Balance (Trackster or 2:05), Nike (Cortez) and Tiger (Corsair).

Women with narrow feet may run into a special problem. Most running shoes only come in men's sizes, which are fine for women with B width or wider feet. The AA and AAA foot tends to slip around in these shoes, no matter how thick a sock or insole is used to take up the slack.

If you are in this situation, and even the narrower models (Adidas SL-72/76 or Tiger Montreal) won't do, don't despair. The American company Brooks has started making women's running flats in narrower sizes. Also, the New Balance Company has all widths available from AA to EEE. The only problem is ordering them by mail. It's better, in general, to try on a shoe before buying.

RACING FLATS

You can race in your training shoes and enjoy yourself, but there's no doubt that the heavier shoes slow you down. If you want the sensation of skimming along at (your own) top speed, light as a feather, rather than galumphing through the miles, you'll want to invest in another pair of shoes just for racing. These models sacrifice foot support and cushioning in favor of lightness. They would rapidly fall to pieces and ruin your legs if worn daily. However, they're fine for short, faster runs once every week or two.

The most popular "racing flats" include Adidas (SL 72/76), EB (Marathon), Nike (Sting), Tiger (Jayhawk) and Tiger (Boston Nairobi).

Two popular racing shoes (because of cheapness) are the Nike Marathon and the Tiger Pinto (formerly the Marathon), which are nothing more than an uncushioned sole attached to a light nylon upper. There is no support or cushioning whatever, and no one other than young high school kids with ankles and legs of iron should try them, in my opinion.

CHEAP IMITATIONS

Once jogging got to be an "in" thing, various shoe manufacturers started adding "speed stripes" to their heavy canvas models and peddling these to innocent would-be runners anxious to save a buck. Many sprained ankles and shin splints developed. Those in the know stuck to Adidas and their ilk, despite soaring prices (the first pair of SL-72s I bought in 1972 cost me $16.95; they now cost almost twice that much and are of no better quality).

In the past year, however, various chain stores have started bringing out quality imitations of the good running shoes. These are constructed of nylon and leather, often with two or four stripes instead of the trademarked Adidas three. And the soles are indistinguishable from the pirated models. These cheap imitations retail for $7-12, a great bargain. After you've worn or studied the expensive brand, so you know what features to look for, I'd suggest checking out the cheapies. I've tried two different models in two months (one Sears and one Penney's) and am very pleased with them.

The cheapies vary in quality, so examine them carefully. Look for the features listed earlier — good cushioning, a firm leather heel support, lightness and so forth. I've found the "made in Korea" models superior to those "made in Taiwan" because of a firmer heel cup, more flexibility at the ball of the foot and lighter weight. One Sears model (Taiwanese) cost $12 but was heavy with a crushable heel cup and a rigid sole — a bummer. Their $7.77 "Jeeper" model with a different stripe pattern and origin (Korea) was outstanding. So look around. Even Safeway has been selling a good training shoe (four-stripe at present).

Don't be worried by the super low price and conclude that such cheapies will inevitably ruin your legs. Rumor has it that even Adidas are now mass-produced in Taiwan or neighboring countries and cost $3-4 to put together. The *name* is what gives them a 900% markup, not the quality. Even $7.77 probably gives Sears a good profit.

If you use plastic or leather orthotics (foot supports), which can be switched from one pair of shoes to another, this will solve the problem of the often inadequate and erratically placed arch supports in the "cheapies" I've seen. Or you can remove the original insole and replace it with a Dr. Scholl's or one of your own invention. Experiment.

SHOE REPAIR

Whatever kind of shoes you buy, after a few hundred miles they'll be in need of repair or replacement. But it gets expensive to buy new shoes every few months, and in most cases you can make the shoes last a couple of thousand miles if you repair the soles faithfully as they wear down. The uppers take much longer to wear out, which is fortunate since they are harder to fix.

Most runners wear down their soles fastest at the outer

corner of the heels. This is where the foot hits first in a normal stride. Just a little wear, an eighth- to quarter-inch, is enough to throw the foot out of alignment and lead to knee problems (usually a pain on the outside of the knee or under the kneecap). So keep your shoes built up *level* (don't over-compensate so you tilt inwards) at all times.

Various goopy substances are available, which you can just smear on and let harden. Something called "Goo" is advertised in tennis magazines, and "Sole-Saver" in runners' publications. Both are easy to apply — like peanut butter — but wear down fairly quickly. Somewhat harder and longer lasting is "hot-melt-glue" which you apply with a special glue gun. I've kept about eight pairs of shoes in circulation far beyond their natural life span thanks to this glue. The only drawback is that you tend to make clicking noises as you run, once your rubber soles are reinforced with hard glue.

If you have time and care to do a proper job, the best and longest-lasting sole patch is one cut out of old truck tire inner tube (ask at your local garage for some scraps). You cut this to size with scissors, shave it with a knife to match the taper of your worn area (if you want to be fancy) and apply it with contact cement — the kind you smear on both surfaces, let dry (until tacky), then clamp together hard.

These patches are virtually indestructible. I used a naturally galvanized hunk of inner tube I found while driving through Death Valley. It had been baking in the heat for Lord knows how many years, and the rest of my shoes wore out long before the patches. The only trouble is that the cement bond sometimes gives out under the stress of countless footsteps and you have to reglue.

If you are a real artist with great attachment to a particular pair of shoes or if you're really cheap, you can patch the uppers as well, using leather (or nylon) scraps and the same contact cement.

Finally, for about half the price of a new pair of shoes (currently $12.95), you can take your old faithfuls to a Tred-2 dealer (or send them in) and have them put on new soles just like the originals. For the price, Tred-2 will also stitch and repair the uppers, replace shoelaces and so on.

You have to specify what you want or don't want. Just before the Boston Marathon in 1974, I got back my favorite marathon shoes from which I had carefully removed the cotton insole so I could use a Spenco neoprene insole instead. Alas, Tred-2 had carefully glued in brand-new cotton insoles and I spent about 15 minutes before the start trying to pry them out again.

seven

Clothing

Apart from shoes, what you choose to wear is unimportant. Just wear whatever is comfortable — and preferably loose fitting. As your runs get longer or faster or both, chafing may become a problem and you'll have to experiment with various materials and devices to handle this problem — particularly with bra and shorts.

Before long weekend runs and races, I find it helpful to smear vaseline between my legs, where the shorts might rub, and I use a strip of very light, papery tape called "Dermicel" to cover my skin under the seams and fasteners of my bra, where pressure points can develop. Vaseline also is handy to rub on your toes and feet to help prevent blisters. Any similar lubricant is just as good.

Once I was out running with a fireman, who was not far from the fire station when his shorts began to chafe him badly. We returned to the station, where no one had any vaseline. So he happily smeared heavy pump grease on his legs and was able to run another five miles with no problem.

As for materials, cotton is most absorbent and is good to wear next to the skin to act as a wick for sweat and to reduce chilling. This is especially important in cold weather. Nylon is smoothest and non-chafing — good for shorts and bras. Wool socks and sweaters are a boon for the cold-weather runner. Wool has the useful property of retaining warmth even when soaking wet. It acts sort of like a wetsuit.

Here are a few suggestions that I've solicited from women runners all over the United States:

Shorts. You may make do with men's nylon track shorts, worn over a cotton or nylon brief. I'm told the "Ron Hill" style that is cut high over the hip is especially comfortable. The sizes and fitting are not ideal for women in any of these men's trunks, however.

I and many of my friends who run from a gym with a swimming pool have adopted Speedo men's swim trunks — low cut nylon briefs, two-layered so you don't need underpants.

Any soft cotton shorts are good and usually are cheaper than the fancy women's track briefs sold by specialty shops. And for short runs — up to five miles — go ahead and use your comfortable old bermudas, blue jeans or whatever. Elegance doesn't matter. The only objection to such garments is that they usually start chafing on longer runs.

Bras. Here again, comfort is the only consideration, and chafing is the problem to guard against. If you're small-chested enough to run comfortably without a bra, be happy. This is one less piece of clothing to worry about.

Starting somewhere around a 34-B cup, most women begin to bounce uncomfortably if they run braless. Here a stretchy nylon, one-size-fits-all bra is the kind to use, particularly if you can find a model without hooks, metal strap joints or other complications. Warners, Olga, Tru-Balance and Vassarette all make stretchy, largely seamless models of this type.

If you are large-bosomed, you can still run, but you need more support from the bra in order to feel comfortable. Experiment. Some women like underwire models made of non-stretch materials. Others prefer a heavier stretch material such as spandex. Sears advertises a special "Step-in Sports Bra" in its catalog. I have no experience with this model, but it looks good. Finally, one woman I know finds a maternity bra ideal.

I have read a couple of articles by (male) doctors who, in their ignorance, warned women not go jog for fear of "sagging breasts." This is nonsense. Sagging breasts result usually from overdistention (with fat) which can stretch the skin and break elastic fibers in the subcutaneous fibers. Bouncing will not break these fibers (if it did, you'd see horizontal stretch marks above the breasts, which you don't). The only reason for wearing a bra is comfort. Most women just don't enjoy the sensation of bouncing along madly as they run.

Shirts. Most women who start going to races rapidly acquire an enormous collection of commemorative cotton T-shirts, which are ideal for runs of all distances. Besides, you can impress people as you jog along in your "Bay to Breakers" or "Charleston 15-Mile" or "Boston Marathon" shirt.

In fact, any "marathon" shirt tends to silence smart-asses who might otherwise offer unsolicited comments or advice, like, "Lift those knees." Wearing an impressive T-shirt, you can sail past and enjoy admiring glances instead. The psychological advantages of these shirts are such that you might borrow one for your first few jogs, until you earn your own.

A word about colors: wear a white shirt to reflect as much heat as possible. Use yellow and orange shirts for runs at dusk, so you can be easily seen by motorists. *Never* wear a dark color for night runs or you'll be invisible and in danger of becoming a traffic casualty. Darker shirts are fine as underlayers in cold weather.

Dressing for the cold. Your movement generates enough heat to keep you warm even during Minnesota winters, and women train there throughout the year. Dress on the layering principle. For the legs, thermal underwear or pajama bottoms (flannel) under jeans or nylon sweatpants. For the top, a T-shirt, sweatshirt or wool sweater, topped off by a nylon shell. Wool socks, leather shoes, a ski cap and mittens. If it's so cold that your face freezes, try cutting the top off a ski cap and pulling it down so it covers your neck, mouth and nose, and leaves only your eyes exposed. This wool covering for your face also helps warm the air you breathe.

Rain. In order to keep training, you must resign yourself to running in the rain now and then. If you skip a workout because of bad weather, you'll soon get out of shape, especially in rainy spells.

Nylon minimizes chafing and is best in the rain. Wool socks and leather shoes help avoid blisters from wet feet. Wear a lightweight nylon shell over a T-shirt. Avoid cotton sweats in the rain since they'll absorb water and drag you down. You'll feel heavy and waterlogged after a couple of miles.

Take a hot shower right after running in the rain. Again, your movement keeps you warm, but as soon as you cool off you're in danger of getting chilled.

Rubberized clothing. Avoid it like the plague. This is a gimmick to "lose weight." But what really happens is that the heat you generate is trapped inside the suit and it raises the temperature so you can sweat more. But this water loss is only temporary and you gain it back within hours. More important, the extra heat can be dangerous to your body, especially in warm weather. And in cool weather, the lack of evaporation of sweat can chill you.

Socks. Most runners wear them, simply because it's easier to wash socks than shoes. A clean pair of socks for each run helps prevent blisters, too, by reducing chafing between foot and shoe. Cotton, orlon and wool, usually mixed with some nylon, are all fine. Wool socks are best if you're going to get your feet wet (in snow or rain). They'll keep you warm even when soaked.

For races, some runners — especially marathoners — skip socks because they just add extra weight, and if they fold over or creep down during a hard run they can lead to horrible blisters. This is an individual matter. I find I get blisters *without* socks—probably because my shoes don't fit perfectly.

eight

Diet

Many women take up running to lose weight. I did this myself, having at age 30 become concerned with my incipient middle-age spread. Now, five years later, I must report that I have yet to lose a pound. However, my friends tell me I look thinner, photos confirm the impression, and I have gone from a size 14 in pants to a size 10. So what has happened?

Obviously, I've lost a considerable amount of fat. The typical co-ed contains about 25% fat, the average "older" woman more than 30%. My fat content a couple of years ago was 17% — and I was running less than I am now. At the same time that I've lost fat, however, I've put on some muscle — mainly in the legs, presumably, since I don't do many pushups or other exercises for the upper body. Muscle weighs more than fat. Thus, I've become more compact, losing all sorts of "unsightly bulges," but haven't changed my weight.

My experience is fairly typical of women who are not really overweight when they start running but definitely are flabby. No question about it, the flab goes off in a hurry. But if it's pounds you want to lose, running's not going to do it. You have to *diet*, too.

Dieting may be very mild in nature. It may mean simply not increasing your daily intake. Figure that you run (or walk) off about 100 calories per mile. The heavier you are, the more energy it takes to propel yourself a mile, at whatever speed. So a fat woman may use up twice as many calories as a wee wisp of a 90-pounder, even if they jog together. Chances are, however, that the heavier woman will lose her advantage by eating more when she gets home. Keep track of your intake. The reducing effects of a five-mile jog can be nullified by a donut or two, or a couple of beers.

During the years I've supervised jogging groups, I've been struck by the number of men who come up to me with a smile after a couple of months and complain, "Hey, Joan, I'll have to buy myself a new wardrobe. I've lost so much weight, nothing fits."

They've cinched in their former 39-inch waist to a 30-inch and their pants are baggy. They've lost 20-30 pounds.

I'm extremely envious. So are the other women in the jogging group. Their pants generally are looking baggier by now, too, but the change is hardly so drastic, nor is there usually any weight loss. How do the men do it?

First of all, the men have a beer belly to lose. This makes a dramatic difference. Then they don't put on muscle to compensate for the lost fat, because they usually start with more than the necessary amount. The average male is 40% muscle vs. 23% for the average woman.

Finally, though it's only a matter of speculation, women may eat more to make up for the calories burned up as fuel. Some researchers did an interesting study recently on rats that were forced to run for hours on a treadmill then allowed free access to food. Surprisingly, the male rats ate about their normal, non-excessive diet and lost weight. The female rats cleverly ate just enough extra calories to make up for the amount worked off and maintained that weight.

One hates to draw conclusions about humans from studies on rats (or other animals), but the experiment is one of the few that show a sex difference in response to exercise. And if people react similarly, it would help explain the observed lack of weight loss in the women joggers.

Nonetheless, many of my woman friends who are not such heavy eaters as I am *have* managed to keep their food intake moderate and have lost weight — even as much as 30 pounds — though the usual loss is closer to 10 pounds. Those who lost more generally were overweight to start with — even though they were "normal" according to the standard weight charts.

A word about these weight charts is in order here. You can't trust them. I am 5'9½" and weigh 135 pounds. According to the charts, I could weigh 165 pounds and be "normal." This is nonsense. I'd be a blimp. As a plump teenager, I got up to 148 one year and looked like a dumpling.

The charts simply are based on the *average* weights of the population and the US has an overweight population. So naturally the average is also overweight. A woman in good health generally should aim for a weight *under* the minimum for her height in these charts, regardless of "body build."

The body frame actually makes up very little difference in body weight, maybe a couple of pounds but no more. Muscle content is more significant. Most women are under-muscled since they don't make normal, healthy use of their muscles in most activities. But for all of us, the bulk of weight above the minimum is fat and we don't need that much. About 10-15% is plenty. Fat content above that level, to my mind, is a physiological aberration induced by sedentary living, lack of exercise and overeating.

DIETING

Simply keeping your intake constant while increasing your energy expenditures (three miles per day equals 200-300 calories) will result in gradual weight loss (or fat loss). I figured out once that I should run off 70 pounds every year, according to the miles I put in on the road. Alas, I have a passion for ice cream and peanut butter (the natural kind, just peanuts and salt). After a 20-miler, I make myself the concoction I've dreamed of the last few miles — an orange juice and ice cream blend. This is no way to lose weight. But if you have more will power than I do, or love ice cream less, you won't have to worry about your weight.

For quicker results than the pound-a-week loss which is the maximum to expect by keeping your food intake normal, *reduce* the amount you eat. Eat the same things, but smaller portions. Skip desserts. Don't have sugar in your coffee. No really drastic changes are needed.

If you go on weekend eating binges and are horrified when you step on the scales Monday morning, try a fast. Don't eat anything from Sunday night until Tuesday morning and only drink water, black coffee or tea. Diet beverages just make you hungry, whereas fruit juices contain calories. That's not a fast. A friend of ours (male) couldn't figure out why he didn't lose weight on fasts. Turns out he was drinking a six-pack of beer to assuage his thirst. "Well, hell, that's not eating," he said. Beer contains about 220 calories per can.

Most people will lose 3-4 pounds on this kind of 36-hour fast. Most of this, of course, is water and maybe one pound of fat (which equals 3600 calories). You can run on a fast day and help your metabolism along.

Some runners thrive on longer fasts — 2-3 days, or even a week. I've never tried this and have a theoretical objection. In order to maintain your blood sugar in the absence of food, you burn your own fat and protein. So after a while, you'll be consuming your own muscle protein. Perhaps this only occurs after weeks of starvation, however. Certainly runners who fast up to a week show no signs of deterioration. They just get lean and mean.

One note of caution: when you fast, or if you go on a no-carbohydrate diet, you *must* drink large amounts of water or you may damage your kidneys, which are busy excreting toxic breakdown products of fat. You may also notice a headache after a day or two of fasting. This is thought to be because of DDT and similar toxic compounds which are stored in the body fat and released into the bloodstream when the fat is metabolized. If this is true, you can take comfort in the knowledge that you're flushing the toxins out of your system. You might also take two aspirins and a long run for more specific relief.

One of the chief benefits of a fast, even for one day a week, is that it gets you temporarily out of the eating habit and geared down to a more reasonable level — just the thing for compulsive eaters.

As Dr. Ernst van Aaken points out, "If you don't eat

anything, you can't gain weight." If you're dieting and still don't lose weight, you're still eating too much, however little it may be. This is obvious, but it's amazing how many people, including doctors, forget this basic rule.

FAD WEIGHT-REDUCING DIETS

These fads range from Dr. Atkins' no-carbohydrate diet through so-called "medical" plans which use hormone injections combined with diet. Included in the vast spectrum are macrobiotic, kelp-lecithin-vinegar and fruit juice variations. Dr. Stillman, in his *Quick Weight-Loss Diet,* lists about 50 variations of the one- or two-item diets. There's even a hot fudge sundae diet. That's all you eat for a week. You're guaranteed to lose weight, since you'll quickly lose your taste for hot fudge sundaes and crave something more balanced and healthier.

All these diverse diets will work for a while but I advise against them. That's no way to eat for the long term, and some of the diets are very dangerous. For instance, Dr. Atkins' diet allows you to eat all the protein and fat you like, as long as you skip the carbohydrates. This stipulation results in a very atherogenic diet (one that promotes coronary artery disease). In fact, it's the exact opposite of the diets recommended by the American Heart Association. Despite what Dr. Atkins maintains in his book, a normal person (not massively obese) will have a rise in serum cholesterol and triglycerides (fats) on this diet — a dangerous trend.

Equally important for a runner is that you need carbohydrate as a fuel for your muscles. The average overweight, sedentary American can get along on the Atkins diet for weeks or months and not notice any problem, except perhaps going upstairs. But the runner will start feeling exhausted once her muscle stores of glycogen (carbohydrate fuel) are depleted, which takes about two hours of running. Thereafter, every tiny incline will feel like a mountain. Eat some fruits and breads, and you'll feel restored and will be off this senseless diet.

Dr. Stillman's diet is similar in that it eliminates *all* carbohydrate so you'll feel equally weak on this diet. However, the all-protein diet isn't as dangerous as the protein and fat (Atkins) diet since it promotes the metabolism of your *own* fat (not dietary) and doesn't lead to increased serum cholesterol. And it's designed more for short-term effects, like three days to a week, after which you revert to a more balanced (but low-calorie) diet.

So if you insist on dramatic results, use Dr. Stillman's diet, but be prepared to feel weak. This diet, in fact, is the same as the dreaded "depletion phase" of the "carbohydrate-loading" diet used by many marathoners (described later). It's dreaded because you feel so lousy and weak. Zero-carbohydrate diets were not designed for the active individual.

The "Medical Weight Reduction Clinic" program has been denounced by the American Medical Association, with good reason. This technique combines certain useful features — a 500-calorie diet and daily weigh-in (for motivation) with dangerous injections of HCG, a protein hormone excreted by the placenta and designed to act on the ovaries. What does this have to do with dieting? It is claimed it removes feelings of hunger, but you could get the same psychological effect with injections of water. Indiscriminate use of totally inappropriate but powerful hormones is highly dangerous. The side-effects are unknown and may not show up for years.

The only sensible large-scale diet program I've found is the Weight-Watchers plan. The diet supplies all the necessary nutrients but is low in calories. So if you're overweight and can't reduce by exercise alone, you might give this a try.

HEALTHY DIET FOR ATHLETES

Books have been written about this subject and I won't try to explore it in great depth. See page 154 of this book for suggested further reading.

You should remember that *active* women require more of certain dietary components than their sedentary neighbors. Carbohydrate is one. Most runners find that they naturally tend to reduce their amounts of meat in favor of breads, cereals, pasta and so forth — simply in response to the body's needs.

Thirty grams, one ounce, of good protein a day probably is sufficient, four ounces is more than enough (so there goes your three-quarter-pound steak). Fruits and vegetables are excellent sources of both carbohydrates and vitamins. Extra iron is a must.

Many of my running friends are either vegetarians or natural food freaks. Looking at the blood chemistries of more than a thousand healthy people in my research, I've noticed incidentally that the most ideal pattern (to my mind) is shown by the vegetarian runners. Second best are the sedentary vegetarians, followed by the non-vegetarian runners. All are better, in terms of blood fat and cholesterol levels, than the average, "healthy" American, who seems well on the way to overweight and heart disease.

Since the amount of animal fat in the diet has a profound influence on blood and body fats, the healthier pattern shown by vegetarians is no real surprise. Interestingly, running per se seems to have the same favorable effect. Researchers at Stanford University have shown recently that both male and female middle-aged runners (35-60) have lipid profile patterns generally associated with a lower risk of coronary heart disease and significantly different from that of the average non-runner. So it may not be so much what you eat as what use you make of it in your daily activity.

In general, I agree with Dr. Ernst van Aaken — eat whatever you like, whatever you're used to, but not too much of it. If you're like most runners, you'll probably find your preference shifting slowly in a healthy direction, toward thirst-quenching fruits and juices for instance, rather than fatty hot dogs. Or, as in my case, from Skippy's (saturated fat) peanut butter to the unsaturated, natural kind — a subtle change, but probably significant.

As for natural foods, with all we know now and are constantly finding out about chemical additives, preservatives and the effects of processing various foodstuffs, I think it's just common sense to eat things that are unadulterated as possible. Checking the ingredients label at the store is advisable and may cause you to resist certain appealing items.

Being a chocolate freak myself, I was going to try a nice new coffee and chocolate blend until I read the list of ingredients in order of weight: sugar, non-dairy creamer (corn syrup solids, hydrogenated vetegable fat, sodium caseinate, dipotassium phosphate, sodium silocoaluminate, emulsifiers and artificial color), instant coffee, cocoa (processed with alkali), ammonium carregeenan, salt and vanillian, an artificial flavoring. It was enough to make my hair stand on end.

My young sons used to beg for Ho-Hos, Ding-Dongs and the like as lunch-box fare, until I persuaded them they were craving a mixture of cardboard and Elmer's Glue (plus artificial coloring and flavoring). Reading the labels, it's hard to tell the difference.

While I'm on the subject of natural foods, it's perhaps wise to point out that some eminently "natural" items are not recommended for those weight-reducing or cholesterol-lowering diets. Examples are butter, cream, whole milk, sour cream, cheese, eggs, avocados, coconut and chocolate. You can go to a natural food-vegetarian restaurant and stuff yourself immoderately on a host of fattening and atherogenic (high saturated fat) concoctions.

In your own home, it's good to be aware of low-saturated-fat substitutes for some of the goodies listed. In most recipes, you can use skim milk instead of cream or whole milk, plain yogurt in place of sour cream, cocoa instead of chocolate (I don't know the fat content of carob, another popular substitute). I use poly-unsaturated oil or soft margarine in place of butter, though purists would object that margarine isn't natural, which is quite true. Skip it if it bothers you. Oil is okay. Always check the labels because many brands saturate their pure vegetable oils, thus making them just as dangerous as the animal fats you're trying to avoid. Many companies are downright sneaky about these changes. They'll start saturating, or adding artificial substances, *after* they've hooked the concerned public on their "natural" or "healthful" product. But they're still required to tell the truth (in tiny print, of course) on the label.

VITAMINS AND DIETARY SUPPLEMENTS

With a few exceptions (to be discussed), massive amounts of vitamins are a rip-off. As a physiologist friend once said, they lead to "very expensive urine." In other words, the water soluble vitamins (vitamin C and the expensive B vitamins), if ingested in excessive amounts, are quickly excreted in equally excessive amounts. The body knows what it needs and either doesn't absorb or gets rid of the rest.

Fat-soluble vitamins − A, D and E − are another and potentially more dangerous matter. If ingested in excess, these substances cannot be excreted in the urine to any significant extent. They are stored in the body fat and can reach highly toxic levels. Excess Vitamin A (carotenemia) results in an orange color to the skin (first noticeable on the palms and soles of the feet) and can be fatal. Hypervitaminosis D is less noticeable but can have equally devastating results. As for Vitamin E, which recently has been highly touted as a cure-all, the effects of excessive amounts are not yet known, but some college athletes given larger doses have complained of extreme muscle weakness and fatigue.

Amounts of Vitamins A and E in a normal diet, especially a "natural" one with few unprocessed foods, are sufficient for anyone. Vitamin D is formed in the skin of anyone exposed to sunlight, plus it's added to most milk. Unless you're a non-milk drinker living in an overcast area (Glasgow, Scotland, had the highest incidence of rickets − childhood Vitamin D deficiency − in the whole world), you shouldn't need the supplements. Post-menopausal women may need more than the normal amount, to help prevent osteoporosis. Check with your doctor (but be aware that exercise also helps prevent osteoporosis).

It's hard to hurt yourself with large amounts of Vitamin C and B since they're readily excreted. If you feel more secure taking a gram of Vitamin C for every six miles run, as Dr. Tom Bassler advises, go ahead, if you can find a cheap source of tablets. (It's impossible to eat that many oranges.) Personally, I think it's unnecessary and useless. I do take 500 milligrams (one-half gram) daily, which is almost 20 times the recommended dose! I figure it may help protect me against colds — though there is no good evidence that this is so — and it won't hurt. There is some indication that runners also lose a lot of vitamins in the sweat (and the urine) and may need a little more than average amounts of C and B for this reason.

The B vitamins are expensive but sell briskly since the deficiency diseases such as beri-beri and pellagra are well publicized. Beri-beri is sometimes seen in old alcoholics and other derelicts, but is no more of a problem in the average middle-class American home than is scurvy. (Unfortunately, deficiencies in poorer families that subsist on lower quality and "junk foods" are a serious medical problem.) Adequate protein intake generally insures enough Vitamin B. But if you want to be on the safe side and like the taste of wheat germ, sprinkle it on your morning cereal (along with bran for roughage and raisins for iron) and you'll feel comfortable.

One food supplement I recommended for all women who are still menstruating is iron. Iron deficiency is extremely common in women and especially in those in the 30s and 40s. Childbearing causes a tremendous drain of iron reserves already depleted by years of monthly blood loss. *The American diet does not contain enough iron to replace what is lost.* Even if you eat oodles of liver, spinach and egg yolks, all iron-rich foods, you'll barely manage to keep up. And there may be added iron loss in active women through the sweat.

I strongly advise supplementing your diet with at least a "multi-vitamin with iron" compound. These usually contain 18-30 milligrams of iron (*average* requirement per day, to make up for menstrual loss, is two milligrams, representing the normal 10% absorption of 20 milligrams in the diet). If you are now or have been anemic, you'll need much more (refer to the medical section, pages 117-119.

Be skeptical of the many prophets of vitamin and mineral salvation. There is a human tendency to assume that if a trace amount of something is necessary for health, hence "good," more is better and much more is best. I am worried not so much by this false assumption as the commercial exploitation of fears that somehow one isn't getting enough of some ingredients essential to good health or good running. As Dr. Ernst van Aaken points out, everyone is in search of the magic diet or factor that will make them a great runner. But what makes the runner is the *training*, not the food.

I appeared once on a television program to talk about running. While waiting in the studio, I saw an enormously fat man wheezing his way slowly toward the guest chairs. I feared he would expire of suffocation before he completed the 10-yard walk, but he made it and sank into his chair with relief, breathing heavily. He obviously suffered from advanced emphysema compounded by overeating. Imagine my astonishment when he lit up a cigarette as soon as he caught his breath and chain-smoked (off-screen) all through my interview.

When his own turn came, I learned he was the executive editor of a very popular vitamin-and-health-food monthly which is filled with ads for new compounds, cures and preventives. The editor's topic was pollution, especially air pollution, and how it would kill us. But we could take the right mixture of zinc and other compounds to overcome 40% of the air pollution effects.

I thought to myself that if he stopped smoking he'd eliminate 99.9% of his own air pollution problems. And if he cut his body weight in half, he wouldn't need extra zinc. I'd been skeptical just glancing at this man's magazine, but a look at the man himself confirmed my views. If you see someone like that promoting expensive vitamins and food supplements as the key to good health, and compare him with a lean, non-smoking, physically fit runner, you'll agree that exercise, not food, is the key.

CARBOHYDRATE LOADING

This special diet has been used by many world-class marathoners in the past few years, as well as by many more humble long-distance runners trying to get a "personal best." Let me say at the outset that Frank Shorter, the Olympic marathon champion in 1972, *doesn't* use it. Nor does the world's premier over-40 marathoner, Jack Foster of New Zealand (who ran 2:11 at age 41). Jack just eats carbohydrates all the time.

Seriously, no one knows if the diet works or not. Some swear it improves their performance, others don't think it makes any difference. Most of us have had both good and bad races using the diet, and not using the diet. But you'll hear of it and may want to try it if you're a marathoner. Women, theoretically, may need it even less than men.

The diet is based on the concept that glycogen — muscle starch — is the primary fuel for muscle contraction (under certain conditions which may not apply to the marathon). The average store of glycogen in the muscles is exhausted after 1-2 hours of steady, hard work (the original experiments were done with subjects on an exercise bicycle). This diet has been demonstrated to increase the stores of glycogen in the muscles — sometimes by 50% or more. What has not been so clearly demonstrated is that the larger amounts of glycogen lead to improved distance running performance. The evidence purporting to show this improvement of running time for an 18-mile race (average time 1:40-2:00) applied only to the *untrained* runners studied. The fastest, better trained runners didn't show the effect (see the discussion "Fat as Fuel," pages 91-96).

The diet itself is simple. Run long — two hours or more — one week before the big race. This will deplete your glycogen. During the next three days you keep the glycogen low by (a) continued running and (b) very low carbohydrate intake. For best results, use Dr. Stillman's diet of cottage cheese, eggs, lean meat and so on, plus a little lettuce for variety, though it has some carbohydrates. You'll feel weak, clumsy and generally lousy for these days. Then (joy of joys) you restore carbohydrate to your diet — pasta, potatoes, breads and fruits (go easy on the candy and cakes or you may make yourself sick). Run very little so the glycogen being formed by your muscles isn't used up.

The initial depletion followed by carbohydrate starvation

causes the muscles to supercompensate and form larger than normal amounts of glycogen. Some researchers believe you can get the same effect by running to depletion (exhaustion) four days before the big race and then loading carbohydrates immediately, thus skipping the horribly unpleasant protein days. However, you may gain excess weight (lost during protein days) and the originators of the diet claim you won't store as much glycogen.

A few warnings: This diet causes quite an unnatural load on your system and should not be used more than once or twice a year. Furthermore, your body adapts to it and won't respond with the wanted rebound after the first few times (especially if you use it too frequently). And you are rather susceptible to accidents and illnesses during the protein days.

Finally, the diet is useful, theoretically, only for races long enough to deplete your glycogen — in other words, 1-2 hours or longer. Most people think two hours is the usual time and that glycogen depletion is responsible for the notorious "wall" that runners (generally male) encounter at about 20 miles of the marathon. So don't carbohydrate-load for an important race of, say 10 kilometers. It's useless.

Once I met a college coach who misunderstood the diet and had his entire team — sprinters through milers — on the diet every week of the season. The cafeteria served all protein dishes to the team Monday through Wednesday, high carbohydrates thereafter. I'm surprised the team didn't rebel, but they were probably too weak.

nine

Safety

Is running safe?

Until recently, I would have answered this question with an unhesitating "yes." I never felt that a running female, huffing along sweatily in her oldest clothes, seemed like much of a sex object. Furthermore, I had the idea that lurking rapists would look for a more slowly moving target, like a walker.

In the past few months, three of my friends have been attacked in three different US cities and I've been forced to the reluctant conclusion that no urban area is safe for a lone female nowadays. Rapists are not really after sex. Violence and domination give them their thrills, and if a 90-year-old withered hag is at hand, they will just as soon assault her as a prom queen. The violent and destructive nature of the attack is the same in both cases and the little old lady probably would be less of a handful.

There are certain elementary precautions every woman should take when she runs. If you live in Vermont, Maine or Montana, you're probably safe and can skip this section. Otherwise, read on carefully.

All three of my friends were attacked from behind, two of them in broad daylight. Both national class marathoners, they were out on training runs in areas much used by joggers, so on hearing footsteps behind them both women felt semi-amused at "another fragile male ego" intent on passing a mere woman. Next thing they knew, they were grabbed by the neck. Fortunately, both of these women escaped unraped by fighting back, struggling or screaming. The third, attacked at dusk in a deserted area, was not so lucky.

Needless to say, all have learned one of the cardinal rules for running women.

1. *If you hear footsteps, look behind you.* Don't assume it's a friendly runner overtaking you for a chat until you've checked him out. If he's wearing expensive running shoes, chances are you're safe, because rapists don't go in for $20 pairs of shoes. If he's in sneakers or Hush Puppies, dash across the street — he may be a fake.

2. *Try not to run alone anywhere* — not even in a well-populated area if there are gaps in traffic or nearby bushes you could be dragged into. Another woman is adequate protection. A man makes you feel even safer, and groups are both fun and safe.

3. If you must run alone (and we all have to at times or we'd never stick to a regular running schedule), *stay away from dismal, dark or lonely places.* Keep an eye out for suspicious men loitering near bushes and cross the street to avoid them if necessary.

4. *Carry a weapon.* The simplest I know, and the only legal one, is a small (four inches long, one inch in diameter) can of dog repellent called "Halt." It is similar to Mace, and you can spray it in the eyes of attackers of the canine or human variety. Look for this in bicycle or other sports shops.

Finally, if all the above seem ominous, remember a woman *walking* alone is more likely to be attacked than a woman running. Just try not to run alone anywhere you wouldn't feel safe walking. Unfortunately, this territory now includes large chunks of most US cities.

Part III

Running Medicine

ten

Physiology

Traditionally, women have been known as the "weaker sex." When it applies to weight-lifting, this characterization is generally accurate. But let's consider a few other situations where women hardly can be considered weak.

Throughout the world, women live longer than men. Their average life expectancy is 3-5 years greater. Women bear the strains of pregnancy and childbirth, often repeatedly. Among the survivors of shipwrecks, mountaineering and similar disasters, women generally outnumber men, apparently because of greater tolerance of cold, exposure and starvation. As for endurance in sports, many of the world long-distance swimming records are held by women.

The above evidence suggests that, in fact, women are tougher than men. Endurance rather than power seems to be their natural strength. So it seems ironic that official regulations for many years limited women runners to sprints. Races of 800 meters and up for women are comparatively recent phenomenon, and permission for women to run the marathon, 26.2 miles, only was granted by the AAU in 1972. The progression of world records in the longer distances has been phenomenally fast since 1972.

Women are obviously physiologically different from men. However, only a few of these differences affect athletic performance. The difference in muscle mass, hence strength, is most obvious. The average female is 23% muscle (by weight) vs. 40% for the average male. Conversely, women have more fat than men (25% vs. 15%) for untrained women and men, 15%

vs. 5% for trained runners. The female bone structure is lighter, and fat weighs less than muscle. Therefore, a woman usually will weigh less than a man of the same height, and also will have less power to propel the same mass. It is for this reason that the women's mile record will never equal the men's. The mile run, like sprints, requires power and speed—muscle-dependent attributes—more than stamina and efficiency of movement. It is in the latter characteristics that the average light-framed, slim female runner excels.

It should be noted in this context that the typical female's lack of strength in the upper body is more a function of disuse than of biology. Dr. Jack Wilmore of the University of California at Davis studied a group of co-eds in a weight-lifting program. (He recruited more co-ed volunteers for this course when it was billed as "body shaping through weight training" than when it was simply "weight-lifting for women.")

Dr. Wilmore found that the women could increase their strength 50-75% without any increase in muscle bulk. So female fears of developing "bulging, unsightly muscle" seem unfounded in physiology. Muscle bulk appears to develop in the presence of large amounts of androgenic hormones. So women, with only low levels of circulating androgens, can increase strength dramatically without appearing "musclebound." This observation should be a great boon to potential Little League pitchers working on their throwing arm, as well as to girls who wish to try field events without sacrificing their slimness.

The difference in muscular development reflects a hormonal influence, as does the distribution and utilization of fat. There are numerous hormonal differences between men and women which have not yet been studied. This is uncharted territory, but we can assume that the effects on athletic performances are enormous and can be to the advantage of women. For a discussion of possible feminine (hormonal) superiority in fat metabolism, see the following discussion of "Fat as Fuel."

Women tend to be handicapped by a final physiological factor—their lower red blood cell count. Since the hemoglobin in red cells transports oxygen to the tissues, it follows that most women won't be able to carry as much oxygen as men, and on this basis alone will generally have a lower aerobic capacity. Aerobic capacity usually is defined as the maximal oxygen consumption—the amount of oxygen used during a "maximal" but brief exercise session on the treadmill, bicycle ergometer or whatever. It is expressed as milliliters of oxygen per kilogram of body weight per minute.

Dr. Wilmore has found that top women runners have high maximal oxygen uptake and these values, if expressed as milliliters per kilogram of *muscle* (rather than body weight), are similar to those of top male runners. However, the values would probably be still higher if more hemoglobin were available.

Add to this lower hemoglobin the fact that many women are chronically iron deficient because they don't replace the monthly blood loss (see "Anemia," pages 117-119) and you get a limit on oxygen carrying capacity which can seriously reduce running performance. I think all women should take a daily iron supplement to make sure their bodies will manufacture as many red cells as possible. Still, it would take the equivalent of a "blood-doping" transfusion of at least a pint to put the average woman on a par with the average man.

At least one authority on long distance running is convinced that women's physiology gives them an *advantage* over men in long races. I explored this theory propounded by Germany's Dr. Ernst Van Aaken, in the December 1974 issue of *Runner's World*. That article is reprinted as the next chapter.

eleven

Fat as Fuel

Something very peculiar seems to be happening with women long distance runners. A few examples:

● Eileen Waters finishes her second 50-mile run at a pace of 6:30 per mile, running faster by then than any man on the track. And she isn't in pain like so many of the men. She crosses the finish line to set a new world record of 6:55, smiles and exclaims, "Oh, I feel so great!"

● Miki Gorman, looking fresh after her victory (in 2:47) at the 1974 Boston Marathon, says to the TV interviewer, "I can't run much faster, but I can run much, much farther. Once I ran 100 miles on the track." (The inverviewer looks at 89-pound Miki in obvious disbelief.)

● Natalie Cullimore, in the 1973 Pacific AAU 100-Mile Championship, outlasts all the men in the field and wins in 18 hours—two hours slower than her best time but two hours faster than the only male finisher.

While I was in Germany in 1974, having tea and chatting with Dr. Ernst van Aaken—doctor, biochemist, coach and lifelong promoter of women's distance running—I mentioned these feats and wondered what was the secret of the women's extraordinary endurance.

The doctor answered immediately, "It's simple. They are running off of their fat."

This was a totally new concept to me (especially since, like many women runners, I am frequently dieting to get rid of fat). I eyed my apple cake dubiously and ventured to ask, "But what about glycogen?"

Horst Muller

*Women (including Dr. Ullyot, 206) in the first international
marathon: Is fat their secret?*

Dr. van Aaken laughed, "Is that why you are eating carbohydrates? All the glycogen you could possibly store would only last you for 30 kilometers (18.7 miles) at the most. A simple calculation shows that. All that apple cake won't help you on Sunday (in the women's international marathon). It will simply add to your weight."

Well, I finished my apple cake without choking, but determined to find out more about fat metabolism in running. First, I conducted an informal poll of all the leading women marathoners gathered in Waldniel. None of them, surprisingly, had ever "hit the wall" in a long race. This unpleasant phenomenon is far more common among men.

Several explanations are possible, the simplest of which is psychological. Generally, women run more for enjoyment than to "prove themselves." Thus, women don't usually bash along at high speed and burn themselves out or quit when they fall off the pace. This is true, but the explanation of this different behavior may be physiological as well as psychological.

"Hitting the wall" is generally considered to result from glycogen depletion. Thus, various special carbohydrate-loading diets, designed to postpone the moment of truth by increasing glycogen stores, are in vogue. However, fat is always available as fuel, and perhaps women are better at utilizing it. (At present, this suggestion is purely theoretical.)

In the American and Scandinavian preoccupation with glycogen, the important role of fat has been overlooked. Fat in general is regarded as so much dead weight to carry about. Excess "depot fat" acquired by overeating is just that. However, much of the body's fat—especially that stored by trained long-distance runners—is highly active metabolically and serves as a superior fuel for endurance performance.

Adipose tissue has a much higher energy yield per gram than glycogen (7:1 ratio), is easily stored in the various nooks and crannies of the body, and, in fact, is preferentially—almost exclusively—burned by migrating birds and other species that must cover long distances. The principle endurance muscle of the human body—the heart—also burns fat in preference to all other substances.

Classic experiments by Christensen and Hansen in 1939 showed that during *submaximal* (aerobic) work up to three hours, fat normally contributes as much as 70% of the energy requirement. The ratio of fat to carbohydrate used as fuel increases with longer exercise. Also, the proportion of fat used could be influenced by various manipulations—diet, workload and training being the most important.

In brief, glycogen utilization was highest in untrained men working closest to their maximum and on a high-carbohydrate diet. Conversely, a mixed or high-fat diet, lower (aerobic) workload and, most importantly, long distance training increased the proportion of fat burned—up to 90%. In other words, the working endurance muscles became more like the heart.

Recent animal experiments by Holloszy in the US have

shown that training will almost double the amount of myo-globin, mitochondrial (respiratory chain) enzymes, and the various enzymes involved in the breakdown and oxidation of fat within the leg muscles.

A Swiss researcher named Howald did muscle biopsies of well-trained male 100-kilometer runners and found an average of 22.3% fat mixed in with the lean leg muscle. This compared to about 10% in untrained men and in lean distance runners trained over shorter distances. (Fat contained *within* muscle is not to be confused with percentages of total body fat, which is low in all runners.)

The distinction between active, "trained-on" fat and passive, "eaten on" fat is very important. Only the former is useful. Otherwise, as Dr. van Aaken points out, the best eater would be the best runner.

In order to develop the capacity to use one's fat efficiently, he says, one should run daily over long distances (10-40 kilometers), always aerobically—slowly. Caloric intake should be limited to 2000 per day, including 50 grams of unsaturated fat, and runners should take regular fasts. Using this training formula, Dr. van Aaken predicts a men's marathon time of under two hours, and for women times under 2:20.

Granted that the oxidation of fats in running is much more important than most of us have realized. What does all this have to do with women? To begin with, even well-trained women usually have about 10% more fat than similarly trained men. Much of this fat is subcutaneous and serves as useful insulation.

More of the women's total body weight is stored fuel and correspondingly less is dead weight, i.e. muscle. Dr. van Aaken emphasizes that the average woman is 23% muscle vs. 40% in men. Thus, women have a hormonally-determined sex-linked disadvantage in muscle dependent activity such as sprints or shot put but a corresponding advantage in endurance activities. In running, it is naturally important to be as light as possible—witness Miki Gorman—and muscular men are more handicapped than helped by their bulk over long distances.

Nina Kuscsik was one of the first to show how fast women can run. Here she runs in Indiana's Marathon.

In effect, then, women are built for distance running and will always do better, relative to their own capacities, where endurance rather than power is important. Eileen Waters again provides an impressive example. In a 1974 marathon, she ran her best time of 3:03 (average of seven minutes per mile), starting out at 7:30 per mile and ending up at 6:30.

Aside from the rather startling increase in speed with distance, this doesn't sound so remarkable . . . unless one knows that Eileen's best mile time is about 6:20. An equivalent performance by Frank Shorter would have him run 5:15 per mile for the first half of the race and finish at 4:15, averaging 4:45 for the whole run.

Eileen and probably other women obviously don't "run out of glycogen" and grind to a halt as so many men do. Several explanations are possible (and speculative):

1. Women not only contain more fat (fuel), but they may know how to use it more efficiently. Possibly their enzyme systems are more geared to oxidize fat. As far as I know, all studies of fat vs. carbohydrate utilization have been confined to men—or male animals. It would be interesting to have some data on women—milers, marathoners and untrained.

2. Women may burn a higher percentage of fat, thus their available glycogen lasts longer and they feel better. This is quite possible even in the absence of sex-linked enzyme capabilities, since the more aerobically anyone runs, the higher the percentage of fat utilized. Glycogen seems to be reserved more for the anaerobic "heavy work." A man can easily run so fast that he uses up all his glycogen at twice the normal rate, and crashes early. By running aerobically, one can perhaps burn a better mixture of fuels.

The ideal long-distance runner has been defined as a strong engine (heart) inside a light frame. The average woman will have a lighter frame than a man of the same height and an equally strong engine, since male and female hearts are equally responsive to training. But women may illustrate a third desireable characteristic: the ability to utilize "high-octane" fuel in the form of fat.

REFERENCES

Astrand and Rodahl, *Textbook of Work Physiology,* McGraw-Hill, 1970 (especially Chapter 14, "Nutrition and Physical Performance).

Pernozand Saltin, eds., *Muscle Metabolism During Exercise,* Plenum, 1971.

Van Aaken, "Kann man die Ausdauer durch einseitige Kohlenhydrat-Diet steigern?" (available from author, 4056 Waldniel, Richard-Wagner Platz 5, Germany).

twelve

Injuries

Unless you are extremely lucky and overflowing with more than your share of common sense, injuries are inevitable at some stage of running. This is because in order to get into condition—and later to improve it—you must apply a certain degree of stress to your body. Not just more than the everyday demands on heart and lungs, but also stress on joints, ligaments, muscles and tendons.

It is very easy to overdo the stress. Usually you won't be aware you've overdone it until you get a sprain or a sore knee or fatigue fracture, all of which I have had more than once! Injuries generally occur when you're feeling good and running well. You push a little harder and there you are, laid up again. It gets monotonous.

A related problem is that different parts of the body respond to stress at different rates. For instance, you may develop an excellent aerobic capacity—the ability to run easily, even fast, without huffing and puffing—long before your ankles or legs are up to that pace, so that your stiff or sore legs hold you back. Conversely, if your legs feel fine, you may be unable to break six, seven or eight minutes in the mile because you haven't yet developed wind for it.

Fortunately, since most injuries result from relative overstress (overtraining), it is possible to prevent many of them by taking proper precautions—the right shoes, the right choice of distance and pace, taking care not to progress too fast in your conditioning efforts or marathon training.

For this reason, when women joining our Institute-sponsored

jogging groups are already in good enough shape (in terms of heart and lung conditioning) to jog a mile the first day, non-stop we discourage them from going farther for at least two weeks. Often they feel so exhilarated after the mile that they want to go three or four with the more advanced group. And they could go the distance, but only the first day! Their overstressed leg muscles would stiffen up in painful rebellion the next day (stiffness is worst two days later). The two-week "holding pattern" at one mile (or two or whatever) is to give the legs a chance to catch up. The longer the legs have been free of the stresses of running—for most women, this means the years since age 12—the longer they need to readjust.

AVOIDING ALL INJURIES

Several years ago, ultra-marathon runner Tom Osler wrote a superb article on this subject (see the booklet, *Encyclopedia of Athletic Medicine)* pointing out the importance of "listening to the body." Though we feel that injuries hit us out of the blue, without warning, the body generally responds to overstress by giving out subtle warning signals which become obvious in retrospect. The most important of these, I reproduce here from his article.

1. *Mild leg soreness.*

2. *Lowered general resistance (evidenced by sniffles, headache, fever blisters and so on.).*

3. *Washed-out feeling and I-don't-care attitude.*

4. *Poor coordination (evidenced by general clumsiness, tripping stubbing one's feet, poor automobile driving, etc.).*

5. *Hangover from previous run.*

These are all symptoms applicable more to the advanced runner increasing her mileage than to the beginner, for whom a period of mild leg soreness is common and usually can be "run through."

The important point is this: If you recognize any or all of the above symptoms, reduce your stress level—cut down the distance, pace or both until you feel refreshed and zestful again.

If you persist in running the same amount with "heavy legs" and clumsiness setting in, however subtly, you'll "accidentally" sprain your ankle, pull a muscle or catch the flu (see chapter on illness, pages 121-122).

To paraphrase Dr. Hans Selye, who first developed the theory of stress, "Stress leads to injury only when it is accompanied by lack of pleasure."

It is wise, too, to remember Arthur Lydiard's rule of thumb. Never to do speed work if your legs hurt. Stick to LSD (long, slow distance), which is the least stressful kind of training.

GENERAL TREATMENT OF INJURIES

Whatever tissue is injured—bone, tendon or muscles—the immediate response of the body to the damage is the same: a local outpouring of fluids and cells release substances that cause an inflammatory response, with more leakage of blood cells and lymph—and the results are the classic five signals: heat, redness, pain, swelling and loss of functions.

Disability can be minimized by keeping the swelling down. For just about any injury, use *ICE*—ice or cold water, compression and elevation. These measures should be continued not just for 15 minutes or so, but over the first day or two, if possible. Put your sprained ankle (or whatever) up on a chair, apply an ice pack and it will be much happier. Even if something is really disrupted—a fracture, say, or torn tendons—this early treatment is advisable.

After things have settled down (this usually takes about 48 hours), the object of treatment is to promote circulation. Now, increased blood flow to the injured area helps remove cellular debris and fluid and hastens healing. Keeping up the compression around an ankle helps. Try an elastic ankle "support" available at drugstores. Such devices aren't much help in other areas, though trainers love to tape legs. If it makes you feel better, try it.

Healing is hastened by heat, massage, gentle exercise and such sophisticated devices as ultrasound. What all these measures have in common is that they increase blood flow. Relaxation is also important since much of the pain of an injury results from muscle spasm around an injury, which may, itself, be very tiny— even microscopic.

Many doctors will want to treat you with the big guns—cortisone injections, butazolidine pills, valium for "relaxation." In a word—*don't.* Cortisone makes you feel good and takes away the pain—temporarily—so effectively you're liable to injure yourself further. Moreover, injections into tendons will eventually weaken them and can result in complete rupture if used too extensively.

Butazolidine is an anti-inflammatory drug whose superiority to simple aspirin has never been demonstrated. It is most effective in rheumatoid arthritis and is not recommended even in other forms of arthritis, and certainly not in trauma or overuse injuries. Butazolidine is a dangerous drug with unpleasant (and sometimes fatal) side-effects. Steer clear.

Valium may be the most over-prescribed drug in America. Doctors hand it out like candy to nervous or depressed patients. Sure, you'll be both nervous and depressed for a while if you're grounded from running. But resumed activity will cure this. As for muscle relaxation, valium does help but so does aspirin.

Personally, I think aspirin is a very useful and much underrated drug. Unless you're allergic to it, try 2-6 tablets a day for any inflammation (bursitis, tendinitis, periosteitis and so forth). Dissolve them well in milk or juice to minimize stomach irritation. In fact, it's best to take them at meal time (*and* dissolved). I recommend aspirin *not* for pain relief, but for its anti-inflammatory action and for muscle relaxation. Both effects hasten healing.

SHOULD YOU RUN WHILE INJURED?

Unless there is a complete discontinuity at the site of injury (as in a fracture or ruptured tendon), there is really no need to keep the part immobile during healing. In fact, just about anything that increases blood flow to the injured part will promote healing, and exercising the limb is a very effective way to stimulate the local circulation. (Other measures include heat, ultrasound, massage and combinations of these such as whirlpool baths.)

To exercise an ankle, knee or leg muscle, it is not necessary to run. You can bicycle, swim, hike and walk as much as the injury will permit. But if you're like most runners, you'll be longing to return to your favorite trails and not just at a walk. So, after the first few days of ice treatment, try a gentle jog and see how it feels. If it's excruciating within 100 yards, *don't* grit your teeth and push on. Desist. Walk.

You'll probably feel better after 100 yards or more of walking. If so, try jogging again. You can cover three miles or more fairly early in the recovery period if you use this walk and jog technique. There is nothing disgraceful about interrupting the "run" to walk whenever you need to. You'll recover faster, whereas if you force yourself to run a set distance, you may cause further injury.

This is a hazard because until you are fully recovered, you'll probably be running with a limp—or at least making subtle adjustments in your gait to protect the injured part. You may not even be aware of pain, but if you're limping, your body is still protecting you. And the abnormal gait puts unusual stress on all sorts of muscles and ligaments you won't know you had until they begin protesting. So do plenty of walking when it seems indicated.

Dr. Ernst van Aaken has treated thousands of runners with this walk and jog approach. He is a firm believer in what he calls "non-protective therapy," by which he means therapy that uses the injured limb in order to restore it to full function.

From experience with my own injuries, comparing the effects of a complete lay-off (as recommended by 99% of American physicians) and judicious but early return to activity (within a few days to a week), I can testify that my recovery was much faster with the van Aaken method. I lost some speed and racing capacity, but not my general conditioning. And I was in a much better humor during the periods of reduced training if I could just get in 2-3 miles a day "for mental health."

Next time you hear a friend complaining that she hurt her

leg, laid off a week, didn't get better, still hurt after a week or so, laid off three weeks or six weeks and still not better, you might suggest that since rest didn't help, she should give exercise a try. It's heretical and few doctors would dare suggest it, but it works.

thirteen

Treatment

SHIN SPLINTS

This is a vague term, but you'll usually know if you have them. It occurs most commonly in beginners and in those who suddenly change running surface (therefore style). "Shin splints" means pain in the front of the leg. Press along the shin bone, laterally. If you say "ouch," this is your problem.

Causes. Obscure, but probably related to improper or excessive toe action while running, since the sore muscles (and adjacent, inflamed membranes) control the toes and lift the foot (dorsiflexion).

Treatment. In beginners, shin splints come from (1) improper shoes (those old, cherished Hush Puppies, loafers or sneakers are *not* good running shoes); (2) toe-running. Both problems are easily corrected. While recovering, run on soft surfaces if possible, use aspirin, rub with Ben-Gay or similar compounds. If shins are very painful *after* a run, apply ice for a while.

More advanced runners shouldn't have the problems of shin splints unless they change foot gear or running surface too abruptly. If you've been a road runner for years and suddenly switch to running barefoot on the beach, watch the mileage for a week until your legs get used to the switch. The same applies if you're switching from sand or grass to the road. It's best to mix the different kinds of running for several weeks.

The same principle of gradual transition applies when you change your training pattern. If you introduce hill workouts or intervals, do so a little at a time. Beware especially of hard, indoor tracks, which have ruined many shins, achilles tendons and so forth.

A good exercise for shin splints is to stand on the edge of a bath towel and try to gather it up with your toes.

SPRAINS

Yes, you can sprain your ankle without knowing you twisted it. If the ankle swells badly, hurts and is tender, especially around the outside and under the ankle bone (lateral malleolus), and if you've been running less than three months, you have what I call "beginners pseudo-sprain" ("pseudo" only because it is not caused by stepping in a hole and rupturing tendons, but the tendons are definitely irritated, inflamed and sore).

Cause and Cure. Back when we were soft-hearted and let people start our jogging program before spending $20-30 on good shoes, the pseudo-sprain was very common. About one out of three women over 30 got it (including myself). Women who generally haven't been using their leg muscles much since age 12 or so have weak ankles when they start. The ankle joint, like the knee, is stabilized mainly by the muscle and tendons around it. If these muscles and tendons are weak through disuse, they are very susceptible to irritation—as by the jarring of each jogging step or the little ankle stresses and sideward motions associated with the running stride.

Prevention. Prevention consists of protecting the weak ankle until it grows stronger—as it will. Shoes must have well-cushioned soles to reduce jarring, and must either be of leather or have a good leather heel cup. By insisting on such shoes, we cut our "pseudo-sprain" rate to one-tenth of its former incidence in our jogging groups.

The running surface can be hard or soft, but it should be level—no rutted trails or potholed football fields at this stage of training. Occasionally, even the strongest ankles can be done in by cross-country turf, though one is more likely to sprain an ankle when overtrained. I've turned my foot over at horrible angles when in good shape and have been okay again after a few painful steps—no sprain. But when you're tired, watch out on the trails.

Treatment. For "pseudo-sprain," which appears gradually, go right to phase two of general treatment—healing. It's too late for ice, but compression and elevation are helpful at all times. Invest in an elastic anklet (or two—it's good to keep both sides in balance). Put it on in the morning, when swelling is minimal, and keep it on all day. Sit with your foot up and wiggle the foot to get the fluids moving out of the joint area. Make big circles with your toes whenever you think of it. Move the ankle joint. People at work may think you're nuts, but you'll get well faster. You can usually continue to run on a pseudo-sprain, but cut down on distance and speed—and do invest in those good shoes.

The kind of sprain suffered by more advanced runners is usually more severe and can involve ruptured ligaments. If your ankle is black and blue, there has been some real damage. But here, you can use *ICE* effectively and you may wish to consult a running podiatrist or orthopedist, at least to rule out a fracture.

Later treatment is the same, though mobilization must be very gentle if there have been any torn tendons. Tape and elastic anklets are very helpful for support and compression.

KNEES

Knee problems are myriad and can affect runners at all levels. Just as soon as your ankles are strong enough to support the daily run, you're transmitting new stresses up the now-strengthened leg and attacking the next nearest vulnerable joint—the knee.

Take heart, the knee can be strengthened and I recommend especially long, hilly hikes for prevention and treatment of knee problems. But most knee pain, we have learned recently, reflect weak feet rather than weak knees.

Chondromalacia, or "runner's knee," is the most common ailment. Pain, usually under the kneecap, can be associated with clicking noises when you flex the knee and results from irritation and inflammation of the cartilage under the kneecap.

You can have roughening of this cartilage and associated clicks ("mice in the joint") without any pain if there's no inflamma- My own knees are horribly noisy, probably as a result of child- hood knee ailments. But if you have knee pain and visit an orthopedist, you'll end up grounded indefinitely.

A bit of advice: Don't go to an orthopedist unless you have a violent football-type knee injury, like torn cartilage. Orthoped- ists know all about torn cartilages, but have learned nothing in medical school about overuse injuries, or the relationships be- tween the foot and higher portions of the body.

With chondromalacia and with many irritations at the sides of the knees, whether a tendon or a bursa is the painful part, the problem generally lies in improper stresses on the knee be- cause of improper foot plant.

The patella (kneecap) is designed to ride smoothly in a groove between the two knobby ends of the femur (the top of the knee joint). It is attached to the large quadriceps muscle, which is easily strong enough to pull the patella sidewards if the angle of pull is wrong. Result: the undersurface rides over bone instead of in its groove and becomes painful. The cartilage softens, roughens and often thickens. "Chondromalacia" is not a diagnosis. It is merely a sympton of the underlying imbalance.

So look at your shoes and your feet. Look at your running turf. You can get knee pains from running on a slanted beach, the shoulder of a road, around a track (especially the small, flat indoor variety) or by wearing run-down shoes. (Are the heels getting slanted?) All these situations tilt the foot in an abnor- mal plane—and after enough steps, if your ankle is up to the strain, your knee will give out. If the knee is strong, you can de- velop hip pain or back pain. Sometimes I wonder if runners can get headaches from improper foot plant.

If your running ground is straight and flat, and your shoes are perfect, check your feet. Are you flat-footed? Or do you land on the outside of your foot and pronate (flatten down) excessively with each step? All these problems can cause dis- abling knee pain.

Prevention. Build up your shoe heels as they get worn down (see "Shoe Repair," pages 65-67). If running on a beach, track, slanted road or whatever, run half the time in the other direction, or on the opposite shoulder, so your feet aren't always tilted in the same direction.

Treatment. If above measures are inadequate, check your feet. Try arch supports for flat feet and excessive pronation. See a good podiatrist for plastic or leather custom-made "orthotics"—rigid foot supports. When you've diagnosed and treated your foot problem, the knee pain should disappear after a week or so of continued running. To hasten the process, take some aspirin. Don't try cortisone shots or other drastic treatments which are aimed only at the symptoms, not the cause of the pain. This applies doubly to surgery, which, except for cartilage operations, represents the ultimate in drastic and symptomatic treatment.

TENDINITIS AND OTHER INFLAMMATIONS

Tendinitis or virtually any other "itis" can strike your legs at any time. The "pseudo-sprain" which discourages beginning joggers is one form. The achilles tendon trouble that plagues outstanding track athletes and can cause permanent damage is another. All such inflammations reflect an irritation of the structure (muscle, tendon, periosteum, fascia, bursa, joint and so forth) that is hurting. Treatment of acute cases is fairly simple, but the chronic cases may eventually require drastic treatment, such as surgery.

However, I haven't seen nearly as much chronic tendinitis in women as in men, so take heart. I don't know if this good record reflects the fact that women haven't been running as long or as fast as men, or more common sense about early treatment. Time will tell.

How will you know if you have tendinitis? By analyzing the pain and what affects it. Inflammation usually appears insidiously over a period of days. The area is usually tender. (Try squeezing an inflamed achilles tendon and you'll see what I mean.) Aspirin characteristically brings dramatic relief within 15 minutes. Inflammations tend to feel better on motion, worse after prolonged rest. If you get up in the morning and have trouble limping painfully to the bathroom, and yet can get along quite well after walking around the house for a while, your problem is diagnosed.

Though this early-morning stiffness usually involves the ankles and is technically arthritis ("arthro" means joint) rather than tendinitis, the principle is the same. Movement lubricates. This is one malady that is not readily cured by rest. Unless the cause is removed, the symptoms will return as soon as you resume running after a lay-off.

Causes of tendinitis and related ills are many and varied, because inflammation (the source of your pain) is a general response of the body to many different irritants. In one form, a normal tendon is complaining about a new and unusual stress. This is the case in the "sprains" of beginners and in the shin splints (front of leg), periostitis (inside and outside of leg above the ankle bone) and achilles tendinitis often experienced shortly after a return to running following an illness or injury. Sudden changes of running surface, shoes or running style (adding intervals on the track to an LSD base, for instance) can have the same effect.

Treatment of this kind of "transition" inflammation is fairly easy. Use aspirin for the pain and for its specific anti-inflammatory action. Ice packs on the tendon are helpful for a half-hour or so after running. You should keep running or your legs will never adjust. But be gentle with yourself. Don't increase your training load (and thus the irritation) until the pain is gone. If your ankles complain vigorously because you've upped your mileage from 50 to 80 miles in one week, don't go blindly on to 100 miles the next week, even if that's what your program calls for. The schedule must yield, or your legs will get worse instead of better. If you treat your body with consideration and tender loving care when it complains about the new stress, it will adapt. The process usually takes about two weeks.

Similarly, nature will take care of acute inflammation around the knees or hips if these are due to an isolated aggravation. Say you've worn an old, comfortable pair of shoes for a marathon.

Unfortunately, the heels were a bit run down and after 26 continuous miles of fast pacing you've developed a painful knee (usually the outside) or hip. The problem is acute bursitis due to 26 miles of abnormal foot plant in those comfy old shoes. As you limp around, do not despair. Look at your shoes to identify the culprit, then repair or discard same. Take aspirin, apply ice and only jog gently or jog and walk for the next week or two until your pain is gone.

Once I was on a team of seven women who ran in the 24-hour relay, repeating miles on a track for 24 hours. Each of us ran 31 fast miles during this period, or 124 laps, or 248 left turns. Not surprisingly, though, we all wore good shoes, those slanting turns got to us and six of the seven women suffered some leg pain in the following weeks, mostly knees but a couple of hips as well. Those of us with acute bursitis recovered in two weeks but one woman had a muscle strain that bothered her much longer.

I make this point because if you think you've found and removed the cause of the inflammation or if you have a "pain of transition" and are still hurting after a couple of weeks of the treatment I've described, you must look further. Consult a running podiatrist, if possible, or knowledgeable fellow runner. Look at your feet. Are they flat? Or do you run like a duck or pigeon-toed? Do you wear your shoes on the outer border, or the inner heel, or only in the front? All these observations indicate mechanical problems which can lead to inflammation and should be corrected if you want to continue happy running.

In 1975, after having suffered through years of assorted ankle, knee, muscle and bone injuries, I thought I was finally cured—adjusted to all the new strains of my running hobby. Then I developed hip pain which persisted for three months. The usual measures—checking shoes, running on level terrain, judicious use of aspirin—didn't help. So I went to the podiatrist who prescribed orthotics—plastic arch supports which also held my foot in its slightly abnormal landing position. Result—my foot no longer rotated drastically with each step. (I had been unaware of this mechanical difficulty.) After a week of running with the orthotics, I was free of hip pain and had become a True Believer. It's great to find a new cure—this time a mechanical one—for a stubborn inflammation.

A final word about achilles tendinitis, which seems to be the most chronic and depressing of the inflammatory disorders. The importance of stretching exercises in the prevention of this affliction cannot be overemphasized. The calf muscles (gastrocnemius) and attached achilles tendon shorten as they become stronger. Thus each step tugs harder on the tendon and eventually will aggravate it. Practice daily stretching exercises to counteract this tendency.

Stand three feet or more from a wall, keeping heels flat on the ground and knees straight, and lean into the wall. Or stand on a curb and dip your heels. Some people try Earth Shoes, with negative heels, though these can aggravate pre-existing tendon or arch problems, so be careful.

If you've worn high heels for a good part of your life, your achilles may be shorter than normal to start with. If so, be doubly careful in the beginning months and be sure to choose a shoe with a good heel lift, like the Adidas SL-72. If you still feel a strain on the heel cord, add a small heel pad of felt or leather.

Avoid sprinting, which puts unusual stress on the achilles and and all the muscles of the back of the leg. Also, with any kind of tendinitis, you'll find it easiest to run on level ground.

Your foot knows what to expect with each step, whereas on turf or rutted path, the muscles always have to make sudden little adjustments which can be very painful when they involve the inflamed area. Stay on the level and pamper your feet. And whenever your legs get too painful, walk for a while.

MUSCLE PULLS AND STRAINS

These can come on very suddenly, usually during a sprint. If you've been to track meets, you've probably seen some contender in the 100-yard dash suddenly pull up short and step off the track. He has just pulled his hamstring. In distance runners, muscle pulls make their presence known more subtly and tend to involve the quadriceps muscles on the front of the thigh or sometimes the calf muscle. You may notice a nagging sore spot after a long or particularly hard run, or after a hill race if you're not used to hills. It may not be particularly tender to pressure, but certain running motion will become extremely painful, especially as nearby muscles go into sympathetic spasm (to help protect their injured neighbor) and get sore as well. Muscle pulls are the bugaboo of the more advanced runner and often reflect overzealousness in training for some upcoming "big race." If not treated properly, they can lay you up effectively for 1-3 months.

Prevention. Work on flexibility, trying to keep all your leg muscles from tightening up as they normally do with use. Do daily gentle stretching exercises with particular attention to any spots that have given you trouble in the past. A tight, stiff muscle pulls more easily. Warm up slowly and thoroughly, especially before shorter races. If the weather is cold, wear sweats or tights to help keep the leg muscles warm. Hope and pray, and try not to overtrain. If your body is begging for a rest, give it one—no matter what your schedule says. Otherwise, you may miss the big race entirely.

Treatment. When some muscle fibers are "pulled," they will tear and bleed. Initial treatment aims at minimizing the bleeding since this blood causes most of the later pain and disability. Use *ICE* (ice, compression and elevation) as always in the early stages, the first few hours especially. These will stop the bleeding and reduce swelling.

Depending on how effective the *ICE* treatment was, you'll be left after a couple of days with either a small or large amount of blood in and around the muscle. The repair of the fiber takes about a week and you should use the leg only gently in the meantime. If there was considerable bleeding, you'll have a rather messy area of old blood and fibrin cluttering up the injured muscle and interfering with healing. Late treatment aims at increasing blood flow to the muscle so that this debris gets mobilized out quickly. So after the first few days, start using gentle massage, heat and exercise. Whirlpool baths are great, as is ultrasound if you can get it. This focuses the heat and agitation effect onto a small, deep area.

Running will be painful at first, no matter how long you've rested the leg—a day, a week or a month. The running motion will break up adhesions between muscle bundles, fascia (fibrous sheaths of muscles), bones and tendons. A lot of things which should be moving smoothly over each other will have been, in effect, glued together by the injury. Using the muscles will (painfully) loosen them up again. Don't worry at this later stage that you're hurting the muscle by using it. You're doing it a favor and it's hurting *you*—but only for a while, so take heart.

Use your common sense when rehabilitating yourself through exercise. If jogging is excruciatingly painful, walk instead. Whenever the going gets tough, walk. This jog and walk approach to injuries helps them heal faster than if you just sit at home with your leg up. Any other activity—for instance, swimming or cycling, which enables you to use the muscle and increase blood flow without putting weight on the leg, is excellent therapy. Besides, these other aerobic exercises do for the runner what methadone does for the heroin addict. They prevent the worst withdrawal symptoms, though they don't give the same high.

STRESS FRACTURES

Another affliction of the intermediate and advanced runner, stress fractures, occur most commonly in the foot (second and third metatarsals, to be precise). But you can get them in the tibia, femur, hip (femoral neck) and pelvis as well. In the latter two instances, both rare, you'll be a medical curiosity and your X-rays will be discussed at orthopedic "rounds" with much tsk-tsking over your excessive sporting zeal—whether you're running five miles a day or 15. Even the more sympathetic doctors will suggest gently that you take up some less stressful sport—possibly swimming or yoga—and keep your bones intact.

But don't worry, stress fractures heal—usually faster than

regular (traumatic) fractures—and the body adapts as always. Don't fear you'll be a mess of brittle bones all your life. After I incurred probably a total of five stress fractures (two diagnosed by X-ray) in my first two years of running, even I had my doubts, I admit. But in subsequent years I've moved on to more advanced, obscure and exotic problems and even those only occasionally.

Prevention and Treatment. No one knows just what causes a stress fracture. It may be a process analogous to metal fatigue or possibly a momentary imbalance between the bone-forming and bone-dissolving elements in your legs. (Bone is a metabolically active tissue and is constantly remodeling itself to adjust to changing stresses). There's no sudden snap or injury. You'll just be running along and get a sharp pain in the foot (or wherever) or perhaps even just notice a swollen and tender second metatarsal some evening. The fracture itself is generally hairline rather than a break and not usually complete (all the way through the bone). It won't show up on the X-ray for about two weeks. The bleeding and swelling around this tiny crack are what cause pain and muscle spasms.

Again, initial treatment, if you have any warning, is *ICE*. The later treatment is mainly T of T (tincture of time) and continued moderate use as the pain will permit. For a foot fracture, after a week or so, try using a felt arch pad and elastic bandage for support. The idea is to keep the foot bones from spreading (ouch!) with each step and to take the load off the injured metatarsal.

Every-other-day, gentle running will not delay healing (it may even help it) and will keep you from getting out of shape during the 5-6 weeks of disability. Swelling of the foot will increase the pain, however, and cut your mileage down substantially. Be happy if you can do 1-3 miles in this condition. Naturally, if running is too painful despite arch supports and other devices, dust off your bicycle again.

In certain locations, hairline stress fractures can be converted to through and through breaks if added tension is placed on the injured bone. This is a real danger if the fractured bone is just

where a strong tendon inserts, as on the outside of the foot.
Consult a running podiatrist and let him judge whether you
need a cast or not. Some podiatrists know that the only way to
keep a runner from going out and training on the leg is to put
on a cast. Avoid orthopedists, unless you can find one who
specializes in athletes. The accepted treatment for fatigue fractures in the unfit normal American is *immobilization*, so beware.

HIP PAIN

Pain over the lower hip is one of the more gratifying maladies
to treat, because nine times out of 10 the cure is very simple
and fast. In such cases, the pain itself results from bursitis—
inflammation of a small fluid-filled sac (bursa) designed to
smooth the movement of a tendon over the hip. But the irritation of this bursa is usually caused by a simple mechanical imbalance, such as one leg being shorter than the other. According
to some surveys, two-thirds of all Americans have one leg shorter than the other and can reasonably expect hip pain (or low
back pain or even sciatica) if they run long distances with the
resulting misalignment of their hips (one will be lower) and
spine.

Hip pain is one of those problems that arises at the intermediate or advanced levels of running. Minor discrepancies in
leg length won't bother you unless you're repeating the same
compensated (and hip irritating) stride thousands of times
daily. If you go to an orthopedist, he'll X-ray the hip, perhaps
detect slight arthritic changes (many older people have them),
shake his head and advise you to take up some other sport—
like gardening.

Rest, of course, by eliminating the irritation, does relieve the
pain of bursitis. But it will return when your mileage builds up
again. Aspirin, that wonderful anti-inflammatory drug, may also
allow you to run without pain. But if the problem persists, try
the simple cure. Put a heel pad of quarter-inch "orthopedic
felt," or leather, or whatever you like into the shoe on the side
that hurts (right shoe for right hip pain). On rare occasions, the
side that hurts is the longer leg rather than the shorter, so if you

are not cured by the ipsilateral (same-side) lift within two weeks, try it briefly on the other side.

If a pad doesn't seem to do the trick, consult a sports-minded podiatrist for more detailed analysis of your gait and leg problems. There are several different foot and leg conditions—besides unequal lengths—that can lead to the hip tilt which causes bursitis.

BACK PAIN AND SCIATICA

Many pains in the buttocks, hip and leg, as well as the lower back, are symptoms of sciatica, essentially a pinched or irritated nerve root which is susceptible to compression in the lower back and pelvic area. Sciatic pain tends to be sharp, intermittent and shooting, following the course of the nerve down the leg.

Some sciatica, as well as lower back aches, can be caused by the same pelvic tilts and imbalances mentioned under hip pain. Most sciatica, however, reflects a different pelvic tilt, commonly known as "sway back." Dr. George Sheehan has covered the topic of sciatica in detail. Briefly, he feels that most cases appear because the back muscles are strengthened and tightened by running while the opposing abdominal muscles remain relatively weak. The result is an increasing curve in your back and pressure on the sciatic nerve.

Both for prevention of this dismal ailment and for cure, try sit-ups. Don't do the straight-legged, all-the-way-up sort, since these *increase* the curve in your back by the action of the ilio-psoas muscles. Instead, do bent-leg situps. Knees are bent about a 90-degree angle, feet are not hooked under anything (the idea is to keep your ilio-psoas relaxed). Flatten your back against the floor and keep it that way. Put hands behind the head and curl your trunk up from the floor until the small of your back begins to rise from the ground. You'll only be able to curl up to about a 45-degree angle, eight or nine inches off the ground. That's okay. The object here is to strengthen your abdominals and that's as much as they're capable of. From 45 degrees on, the wrong muscles come into play.

Do 20-30 of these "trunk curl" sit-ups daily and you should remain free of sciatica. If you're having symptoms, you can do more, up to 50. Also, sleep on the floor or a bed-board so your back doesn't curve the painful way. Raising your knee up to the chest while sleeping also brings relief. Last but not least, don't neglect stretching exercises aimed at the tight hamstring and and back muscles. Do daily toe-touches (gently, don't bounce), both sitting and standing. Stretch the hamstrings by putting your leg up on a table or chair and bending over slowly toward the foot.

fourteen

Other Questions

ANEMIA

Anemia, or low red cell count, is very common in women of menstrual age. The monthly blood loss depletes iron reserves and the extra demands of pregnancy leave many women with no apparent iron in their bone marrow. Once this iron store is gone, the blood count can drop very suddenly. Many American women are walking about with a hematocrit (percentage of red cells in a volume of blood) of 30-35. "Normal" is 38 or above for women, 40 or above for men. Personally, I think the lower norm for women simply reflects the high incidence of anemia in the population tested to establish the norm. Post-menopausal women usually have a hematocrit above 40, just like men.

Mild anemia is well tolerated, and the average woman may never notice her condition. But get in a situation where you need all the oxygen-carrying capacity of your blood and you'll feel that something is wrong. Anemic women may feel tired, lacking in energy or lacking in stamina as they go about their daily routine. If they start jogging, they can train faithfully and doggedly but they won't progress like other women. They may be unable to break 10 minutes for a mile even after months of daily jogging. When you train and don't get the training effect, chances are nine out of 10 you are anemic. Have your blood checked.

The more advanced runner who is already in top shape may have anemia creep up insidiously. She'll notice very little difference in daily training runs because these are run at a completely aerobic pace, where oxygen-carrying capacity is not the limiting factor. But the moment of truth will come in a race where all systems must be working maximally. The experienced racer will find herself running as hard as ever, but not going anywhere. Her pace may be a half-minute per mile slower than normal, her legs feel heavy and every small uphill grade will feel like a mountain. I know. I've been there. These sensations do not reflect the mild decline that follows a peak. A half-minute per mile slowdown is too dramatic to be in the normal cycle.

If you have the symptoms or diagnosis of anemia, what then? The establishment rule is no treatment until we find the cause — after numerous, fairly expensive tests. However, these tests are unnecessary in most cases, so I would recommend a good trial of iron therapy first. If you don't improve within a month or six weeks, *then* have the tests. Iron is taken in various salts (ferrous gluconate, fumarate and sulfate are the usual forms), one pill (100 milligrams) three times a day. With meals is best, so that the iron is well diluted and won't irritate the stomach. Don't take "sustained release" or "delayed" forms. Iron is only absorbed from the duodenum (upper intestine); it won't do you any good if the iron is released lower. Drug companies don't seem to be aware of this basic physiological fact and push the elaborate form as "less irritating."

Even women who are not anemic should practice prevention by taking one iron pill each day, or at least a "multi-vitamin with iron" pill which supplies 18-30 milligrams, the bare minimum. The normal American diet supplies only marginal amounts of iron — enough for men who don't lose much blood, but not for women. Runners may require more iron than the average American. Perhaps they lose iron in sweat and urine. This hasn't been studied but often male runners show slightly low hematocrits (in the female range) which are restored to normal if they take iron.

The only hazard in taking iron without extensive tests is that you may be masking some other condition. The anemia may not be due to iron deficiency, in which case you won't respond to iron anyway. Or the iron loss may be due to blood loss other than menstrual, for instance a bleeding ulcer or even (rarely) a tumor in the intestine. So if you have abdominal pains or bowel disturbances in addition to anemia, you should definitely have a checkup before starting treatment.

MENSTRUAL PROBLEMS

Should you run during your period? Certainly, unless you suffer such horrible cramps that you're confined to bed. Jogging or vigorous walking generally helps to alleviate cramps. It doesn't worsen them or prolong the bleeding.

Many of my friends find they feel bloated and sluggish for a day or two before the onset of their period. This feeling probably reflects water retention, which can be treated with diuretics (water pills) if severe. Unless you're in an important competition that day, slight sluggishness is no cause for alarm.

A couple of women expecting the pre-menstrual blahs or heavy bleeding during national championships or the Olympic Trials have regulated their period for that month with birth-control pills. Whether this is necessary is debatable. One study of female Olympic gold medal winners showed that top performances were possible at all stages of the menstrual cycle. The benefit or handicap may be more psychological than physical. A questionnaire revealed that most women felt their performance was unaffected by their period. About 20% felt they did worse, 10% better during the period. So the individual variation is considerable.

A few women, mostly beginning joggers, have complained of "cramp-like" pelvic pains during the daily run—not often related to their period. In some cases these may be "mittel-schmerz" or mid-cycle pain. I don't know what causes them, but in most cases these pelvic cramps disappear as the women become better conditioned and continue jogging.

In recent years, as more and more young women have started training with high mileage (60 miles per week and up), another menstrual disturbance has shown up. This is amenor-rhea, or total cessation of periods, for a few months or even a number of years. Unfortunately, you can't count on this phenomenon for birth control. The timing is too erratic.

Amenorrhea may be a response to the low percentage of body fat in most of these women (around 10%), the reasoning of the body being that they are not fat enough to support a pregnancy at that time. Younger women whose menstrual cycles are irregular anyway, and those who have not yet had children, seem most susceptible to amenorrhea. It is not harmful, and periods generally return when the mileage decreases, with weight gain, or just the passage of time. A few preliminary tests indicate that this disturbance originates in the pituitary rather than the ovaries and reflects its overenthusiastic "feedback" control of ovulation.

PREGNANCY

A general rule for any form of exercise during pregnancy is, "Do what you're accustomed to, as long as it feels comfortable." If you've been jogging five miles a day, keep it up. If you find yourself getting tired more easily, cut down the mileage. If your uterus contracts wildly whenever you jog late in pregnancy, walk or swim instead, so there's less jostling.

Not only runners, but horseback riders, ballet dancers and others have all been able to keep up their activity during pregnancy. Using the "talk test" while running, you'll be assured that both you and the baby are getting plenty of oxygen (the baby has first dibs on oxygen, just as it does on food, calcium and iron). The increased circulation will be as beneficial as the continued muscular toning during exercise. Most obstetricians feel that an active mother has an easier childbirth and recovers faster post-partum.

The only condition in which exercise would be contraindicated is "cervical incompetence" — a dilated or weakened cervix — which can cause second trimester miscarriage. In this circumstance, your doctor will order you firmly to avoid any jarring activity. Usually the cervix is stitched to prevent early opening.

Some pregnant women avoid exercise for fear of inducing miscarriage or jarring the fetus loose. Physiologically, this is nonsense. Early miscarriage is now known to be caused by death of a defective ovum or fetus. At all stages of pregnancy the fetus is well protected and cushioned by the amniotic fluid — like fish in an aquarium. Moving the container around does not disturb the floating fetus.

The one restriction I would impose during pregnancy, just to be on the safe side, is no racing or interval work. Theoretically, these activities might result in decreased oxygen supply to the fetus, since the runner is usually anaerobic — building up an oxygen debt, accumulating lactic acid and so forth.

It is not known whether these physiological changes in the mother might adversely affect the fetus — probably not, since Eastern European women have competed successfully up to the fifth month of pregnancy and a couple of women I know have continued track workouts virtually up to the moment of delivery. One even ran a workout during labor. She thought the pains were probably "false labor" and the exercise would make them go away! In all of these cases, the babies turned out strong and healthy. So probably my own bias against racing during pregnancy is unfounded — but I still advise moderation and common sense.

Dr. Ernst van Aaken, having watched many women runners during long careers, feels that motherhood improves performance. He cites the example of Olympic star Fanny Blankers-Koen, who only hit her peak after childbearing. Numerous other examples exist, from Madeline Manning Jackson (800 meters) to Judy Ikenberry (marathon).

Finally, it is apparently perfectly all right to continue running while nursing a baby. There are no problems either with milk supply or with quality of the milk produced. You can comfortably ignore any old wives' tales to the contrary.

COLDS AND FLU

You can run with a simple head cold. The exercise actually helps to clear the nose and sinuses, and you'll feel better after the run. Be careful, though, to keep warm and to run easily so you don't get tired. If your daily stint is a mile, skip it. If it's two miles, cut down to one. If you're used to doing 5-7 miles, just jog an easy three. The combination of continued exercise (which stimulates the circulation) with moderation should restore you to health rapidly.

With a fever, things are more serious. Your body is in a very weakened state, viruses are probably circulating in the blood and it's wise to avoid any additional stress on your system. I never run with a fever. If your heart is skipping beats, as is common in some kinds of flu, all the more reason to stay inside and take it easy. Don't feel guilty or compelled to stick to your present schedule.

I once knew a young boy on the college track team who stubbornly ran a hard workout despite the flu, a high fever and dizziness. Not surprisingly, he fainted when he stood around after the exhausting run. No harm done, fortunately, but he was examined by the school doctor and found to have the typical "athlete's heart" — which few doctors yet recognize as normal for runners. The unfortunate young man was subjected to a whole series of special heart tests and almost catherized before he escaped to a sports-oriented doctor who was able to reassure him. The whole fuss could have been avoided if this runner had only stayed in bed when his temperature was 103 degrees.

"STITCHES"

A "stitch" is a rather sharp abdominal pain, usually located on the upper right side or just under the ribs. It comes on during a run, is relieved by stopping, walking or just slowing down, and is a real nuisance if you are in a race.

The cause is unknown, but is believed to be diaphragmatic spasm most often produced by faulty breathing. The most efficient and relaxed breathing pattern for a runner is abdominal. That is, when you inhale, the diaphragm should descend, pushing the abdominal wall outward. When you exhale, the diaphragm should rise and the abdomen flatten. This is actually the normal way to breathe, but years of concentration on keeping a trim waistline and flat abdomen have reversed the pattern in many of us, especially women. Tell a female friend of yours to take a deep breath. Nine times out of 10, her chest will thrust forward and her abdomen will contract as she expands her rib cage and raises the diaphragm. This is called "paradoxical respiration," and results in stitches if you breathe this way while running.

Stitches are most frequent in beginners and in younger girls who race long distances. Beginners are often tense and have not adopted the more relaxed, abdominal breathing that comes naturally with time and continued running. The young girls, similarly, tend to get tense and anxious on long hard runs and after a few miles of "paradoxical respiration" they succumb to a stitch. You can also induce stitches by irritating the diaphragm with food or drink in the stomach too soon before you run.

The cure is usually simple. For the rare "flu" kind of stitch, wait it out and just jog easily meanwhile. Avoid eating for several hours before the run. For the "faulty-breathing" stitches, practice abdominal breathing at home or on the run. The simplest way to get the hang of it is to lie on your back with a book on your abdomen. Inhale and watch the book rise; exhale and it will descend if you are breathing correctly. It's easier to practice this at home or during a jog than have to learn it in the middle of a race.

ABDOMINAL CRAMPS AND OTHER DIGESTIVE UPSETS

These differ from stitches in being deeper, more diffuse and unrelated to breathing. Cramps tend to make you double up and retreat to the nearest bathroom. They are not relieved by walking.

The cause is almost always something you ate. It may be a food allergy, especially if the cramps come on early in the run. Many adults are allergic to milk. Others react to such things as shellfish, chocolate, strawberries, medication — the list is long. Examine your diet carefully and try eliminating one suspected item at a time, starting with milk, the most common culprit.

If cramps come on later in the run and are accompanied by diarrhea, you may be getting too much roughage in your diet. I've seen this fairly frequently in long-distance runners who adopt a "natural foods diet." After a couple of weeks heavy on the whole grains and fruits, they sometimes find themselves doubling up in a race and dashing for the nearest toilet. The solution need not be to go back completely to easily digestible sweet rolls and other junk food, but to make dietary transitions gradually, like any other change in training.

HEART IRREGULARITIES

"Skipped beats" and other mild disturbances in heart rhythm are not uncommon in runners. I feel them most frequently when getting back into shape after a lay-off, so I tend to regard them as a helpful indication that my heart again is adapting to the increased work load. Others may get these irregularities during heavy training, when they are a good clue to slow down and rest a bit.

Some people never even notice skipped beats. Others get annoyed or worried by the "flip-flop" sensation in the chest that accompanies them. In general, transient and brief periods of irregular beats are no cause for concern and are often induced by too much coffee, Coke or tea rather than too much running. There's no need to consult a doctor for these episodes.

On the other hand, if you should develop runs of tachycardia (rapid beating) or feelings of faintness or sweating along with heart irregularities, do consult a doctor. You may have an allergy to some food or the additive MSG (Accent). These disturbances are not caused by running activity and in some cases even disappear when the heart rate is increased as by exercise.

You should be aware that a well-conditioned runner usually has an "abnormally" slow pulse — somewhere between 40-60, in contrast to the average "unfit" pulse of 70-80. This slow pulse reflects a more efficient heart which pumps out more blood with each stroke, and therefore doesn't need to contract as frequently as an unconditioned heart.

Unfortunately, the unconditioned state is the norm in America, so you're apt to run into unenlightened medical people who worry about you. Reassure them that you're a well-conditioned athlete and that the slow pulse is normal for you. If you must consult a cardiologist, make sure you find one who is familiar with super-healthy people.

VARIOUS RUNNING ABNORMALITIES

In addition to slow pulse, runners may develop a number of peculiarities alarming to the average disease-oriented physician. It is well to be aware of these so you don't get scared to death when you go for your annual check-up and the doctor hems and haws and looks worried instead of congratulating you on your improved appearance and physiology.

Your heart will be large, with a slow, vigorous beat. You may acquire a soft "systolic" murmur which only reflects the larger volume of blood ejected with each stroke. The thicker wall of the heart can cause various EKG abnormalities, including left ventricular hypertrophy, conduction disturbances (heart block, right bundle branch block), S-T segment and T-wave changes. These are all very worrying, to be sure, if they occur in a sedentary little old lady who gets out of breath walking up the steps to her porch. But the same changes are normal for a person with a strong heart.

I cannot emphasize too strongly the importance of consulting a doctor familiar with runners if there is any question about your health. I have seen too many young runners effectively grounded after a school physical which detected a murmur or similar mild "abnormality."

Some blood tests also can be abnormal in individuals who train hard. The most common are elevated serum enzymes and BUN. The elevated enzymes are normally indicative of lung, liver or heart disease, but they also occur with strenuous muscular activity. This last condition is so rare in the US that it is nót mentioned in medical textbooks. As a result, a top Northern California road runner was recently put in bed when he volunteered for a Navy assignment requiring a special physical exam. He had the typical large heart, EKG abnormalities and elevated enzymes of an outstanding distance runner, and thus alarmed his doctors no end. After three weeks in bed, he was deconditioned, out of shape and his enzymes were falling down to the normal level.

"We don't know what you had, but you're getting better," gloated his doctors.

Moral: Beware of the unenlightened physician.

STRESS TESTING

The "stress test," or exercise EKG, has become popular in recent years as screening test for coronary artery disease, an epidemic condition which eventually kills one out of every two Americans. The usual resting EKG only shows the electrical patterns of the heart at rest.

The idea of the stress test is to increase the work of the heart to the point where its demand for oxygen may exceed the blood supply available through narrowed coronary arteries. This relative imbalance of supply and demand, called "ischemia," or lack of blood, causes certain disturbances in electrical conduction that can be detected on the EKG while you're actually exercising on a treadmill, bicycle, steps or whatever device the doctor prefers. If your coronaries are wide enough to supply adequate blood to the heart at maximal or near-maximal effort, the EKG will be normal. It's a simple test, though somewhat costly, and in men it will pick up 85% of otherwise undetected, so-called "silent" coronary artery disease (CAD).

Many runners, aware of the growing incidence of CAD in America, wonder if they should have the stress test as a precaution to make sure they're okay for running races or whatever. Generally, I wouldn't advise it for an experienced runner without special risk factors. Runners' EKGs are frequently "abnormal" even at rest, and you may find yourself grounded by a puzzled doctor before you even step on the treadmill. The demand on your heart if you race regularly is already closer to the maximal than you generally get on a treadmill test. If you're tolerating this, okay, chances are good that your coronaries are up to the challenge.

Finally, there is a certain percentage of false positive stress EKGs — cases where "ischemic" changes are detected on EKG, but subsequent arteriography — X-ray studies of the coronaries — show no narrowing. These "false positives" are especially common in women. Some studies have shown up to 50% "normal coronaries" in women with positive (abnormal) stress tests.

Most good runners who have stress tests are secretly just trying to show off, anyway, to demonstrate to the doctor just how wonderfully fit they are, break all the records and so on. It's a heady feeling. But if you're doing it just for fun, watch out!

The women who should have stress tests, in my opinion, are the previously sedentary beginners who have not stressed their heart for years or who have any of the CAD "risk factors" mentioned in the "beginning" section (Chapter 2). But if you fall into this category, let your doctor decide what tests, if any, are applicable.

ASSORTED FEMALE ILLS

I was prompted to include this section because I read (in a national magazine not known for its insight into female psychology or physiology) an article asserting that jogging leads to sagging breasts, tipped uteri and other problems. The male author, allegedly an M.D., with no other apparent qualifications or expertise, also warned men against a host of jogging ills such as infertility, hernia, "heart-bouncing," varicose veins and fallen arches. If there had been time, no doubt he would have linked jogging to every medical problem known to man, from acne to hypoglycemia.

Such a sweeping condemnation of jogging, unsupported by any evidence, is, of course, nonsense. But since an M.D. wrote it, many people may still wonder uneasily if he's right. So let me, another M.D. and one experienced in the area of jogging, refute at least the pronouncements that most concern women.

Jogging will *not* cause sagging breasts. Breast tissue is a mixture of glandular and fatty components with some fibrous tissue mixed in. The breasts are "supported" not by fibrous ligaments or bands which might be snapped by jogging, but by their internal structure. Thus large, heavy breasts will *always* sag when acted upon by gravity and are best supported by a bra. Lean women, like distance runners, generally have less body fat than the average co-ed and perhaps for this reason tend to be small-busted (though there are a few exceptions). They have less to fear from gravity than the amply endowed woman.

What, then, causes sagging of breasts? Primarily stretching of the internal structure — for instance, by excessive fat or overdistention by milk, silicone and so forth. Aging results in some actual loss of both glandular tissue and fat within the breast, which may then appear relatively drooping — especially if the breasts were very large in earlier years. Neither going braless nor jogging is going to affect the internal breast imposition. Only hormones will do that.

As I mentioned in the bra section (pages 69-70), the reason for wearing a bra is comfort, not prevention of sagging. If you're comfortable without one, fine; if you need a wired corset to keep your 40-D from bouncing around, use it. And disregard what ignorant men with breast fetishes fear about healthful sports for women.

As for the infamous "tipped (retroverted) uteri," this subject has been annoying me ever since medical school. I found that a "tipped uterus" (meaning one in line with the vagina, rather than tilted forward onto the bladder) was considered abnormal and cited as the cause of various female ills such as cramps, infertility, hysteria, headache, "pelvic congestion" and so on.

Yet, I myself, and most of my female friends, had a uterus in the straight ("tipped") position. So do almost 50% of athletic young women, and *all* young girls—in whom it is called a "juvenile" position. The tendency to call such a common anatomical variant "abnormal" and hence undesirable is regrettably frequent in the medical profession. There is absolutely no evidence that a retroverted uterus is associated with higher incidences of the various woes listed than a "normal" or anteverted uterus.

For years, doctors got rich from operations to "suspend" the retroverted uterus in the more proper position. It is not recorded whether the symptoms this operation was supposed to cure actually subsided. During pregnancy, incidentally, the normally retroverted uterus assumes the anteverted position (the only way there is room for it as it grows) — then, following delivery, it returns to its own normal position—i.e., tipped.

I know of no cases where a woman with an anteverted uterus has developed a retroverted, "juvenile" one thanks to jogging. If this did occur, I would assume that as the body becomes leaner and more youthful in appearance, the positioning of the internal organs simply reflects the healthier posture and activity. In any case, this youthful position would certainly not cause congestion, cramps and so on. Those are just old wives' tales — spread, alas, by "old docs."

VARICOSE VEINS

People frequently ask if running is "good" or "bad" for varicose veins. As far as anyone knows, the development and appearance of these veins is not affected at all by running.

Varicose veins result from high hydrostatic pressure in the superficial (saphenous) leg veins. This high pressure, over a period of years, eventually overcomes the elasticity of the veins' walls and leads to bulging and dilatation. The vein structure itself cannot be strengthened, so the logical approach to prevention is to minimize the hydrostatic pressure. If you have a tendency to varicose veins, try to sit with your feet up, wear proper support hose to assist the veins, avoid constricting garters and knee socks. The pressure is increased by standing around without moving, as well as by pregnancy, weight lifting, straining at the toilet and so forth.

Varicose veins tend to run in families. Most people are born with a valve in the saphenous vein at the level of the groin. In the unlucky families this valve is absent — an anatomical variation — so the effective pressure column extends all the way down from the heart, instead of from the groin level.

If varicosities become too painful, or simply for cosmetic reasons, the entire saphenous system can be "stripped" surgically, though the operation is considered somewhat frivolous in this country and is not performed as commonly as in England. The venous blood is then returned exclusively through the deep veins of the muscles, which normally share the load.

During vigorous exercise such as jogging or hiking, the contraction of leg muscles pumps blood vigorously back through this deep system toward the heart, thus temporarily decreasing the load on the superficial veins. This may explain why some individuals with painful varicosities report that the pain is alleviated by regular running.

Part IV
The Results

fifteen

1974 "International"

Sept. 22, 1974, was a banner day for the small West German town of Waldniel (population about 4000). Huge flags of the seven nations represented in the First International Women's Marathon fluttered in the cold wind.

Around the starting line and nearby Sporthalle, crowds like those of Boston milled about, and four different TV stations jockeyed for position with their mikes and cables, tripping up participants and spectators indiscriminately. Hordes of small children dashed around soliciting autographs. Obviously, there was some sort of local competition to see which school child could collect the most signatures in an hour (maximum number being 45, the number of women starting).

Somewhat dazed by all the commotion, the members of the "American Expedition" of nine women stretched or jogged gently along the sidelines, waiting for the noon start. Six of us wore the blue USA uniform, having been designated as the national team on the basis of the National AAU championship in February. Judy Ikenberry, Marilyn Paul, Peggy Lyman, Nina Kuscsik and Lucy Bunz had placed 1-5 in that race. I had only placed 10th, but was chosen as "sixth wheel" since I could also function as interpreter, team physician, manager, chaperone, AAU rep and whatever else was necessary.

Jacki Hansen—the 1973 winner of Boston and potentially the fastest American of all—also was running, as were Masters representatives Ruth Anderson and Catherine Smith. The large US contingent got a tremendous amount of publicity from the Germans, since this was not only the first world marathon competition for women only, but also an official US-German meet, having the blessings of the AAU and its counterpart, the DLV (Deutsche Leichtathletic Verband).

The real star of this historic occasion, however, was a man— Dr. Ernst van Aaken, the famous German physician and trainer who is best known as the "Father of LSD" and coach of German Olympian Harald Norpoth. Not so well known in America is Dr. van Aaken's long-time promotion of women's distance running. He was instrumental in getting the 800- and 1500-meter distances for women and had the previous October sponsored the first national women's marathon in the world, run appropriately in his own home town of Waldniel. The first international marathon, on the same course, was one more tribute to his energy and convictions.

Judy Ikenberry and I, the first Americans to arrive in Waldniel, had been welcomed enthusiastically by the remarkable Dr. van Aaken. Initially awed by talking with a "living legend," we quickly became his good friends, admirers and drinking comrades as the doctor held daily open house for us, over *apfelkuchen,* coffee, beer, ardent discussions of physiology, jokes and music (every now and then the doctor would dash into the piano room to serenade us with a little Chopin or an improvised "March for the American Marathoners").

The energetic doctor, apparently not slowed down at all by the recent accident which cost him both legs, quickly charmed us all with his tireless concern for our welfare and his courage. We also were delighted to find he was as nutty as most runners and quickly christened him the "Closet Dingbat."

During the week preceding the marathon, the Americans were all guests of the OSC Waldniel, the small local sports club which has won 14 German championships. During the days we ate (enthusiastically loading carbohydrates), slept, visited the doctor and ran with two new German friends, Anni Pede and Jochen Gossenberger. Anni, who held the women's world marathon record from 1967-1970, was just beginning to run again after a six-year layoff.

Jochen, the doctor's nephew, is a 100-kilometer specialist.

He enlivened our runs with descriptions of his training methods,
diet (fasting 24 hours before each ultra-long distance race) and
advice on how to manage pit stops on the long runs (in the rain
is best because then you don't really have to stop).

Now, waiting for the race to start, I wondered how the
American marathoners would adapt to the strange situation.
For most, this was the first trip abroad, the first experience of
foreign food and language, the first international competition,
and not least, the first race run without men. There were problems of over-excitement and resultant over-training and fatigue,
jet lag and the unfamiliar diet, in addition to the ordinary con-
cerns of pace, weather and the 42-kilometer course.

Nina Kuscsik looked fresh at the starting line, but she had
been sick the week before and, worse, had arrived in Waldniel
from New York just two nights before the race. Peggy Lyman
had been traveling around Europe for three weeks already and
had gotten a sore throat. Judy Ikenberry, in addition to the
psychological stress of being touted as national champion and
hence the American "favorite," suffered from a small but nagging infection, indicative of depleted reserves.

And Lucy Bunz, wandering around in her long black cloak
which had earned her the nickname of "Batman" or "die
Fledermaus," looked slightly pale. While the rest of the Americans had feasted on homemade pancakes the night before, Lucy
had indulged in her favorite nearly-raw herring, now sitting
like a cold lump in her stomach. "I don't think it was quite
dead," she said, and smiled wanly.

I felt good but so distracted by the commotion, the TV in-
terviews and my constant interpreting and managing duties
that I barely remembered to write my planned splits on my
arm. I was aiming for a 2:58 time, which worked out to 21
minutes for every five kilometers.

I anticipated that there might be as many as 10 women under three hours: seven Americans plus at least three or four of
the Germans and the 19-year-old French runner, Chantal Lang-
lace, who was rumored to have run 2:45 in practice and had

recently raced 2:46 on a short course. Given the competition, the cool weather and the almost flat course, a new world record was a distinct possibility.

But a strong wind had come up during the morning and was to be against us for half of each 10-kilometer loop. Unfortunately, this was the unsheletered half!

The four Americans who had already broken three hours— Ikenberry, Paul, Lyman, Kuscsik—went out together, an exciting sight, four blue jerseys in a row, moving easily at about a 6:30 mile pace. A little farther back were the German and French contenders, along with Lucy, Jacki and I.

As we headed into the wind and the lead pack moved away from the others, I ran beside the German women and Chantal. Christa Vahlensieck, the European champion, remarked that the pace set by the Americans was too fast. Manuela Preuss agreed, saying, "They'll regret it later." Chantal, a small, determined woman, didn't bother with talking, even in French.

The pace seemed reasonable, slightly over 20 minutes for five kilometers, but the German coaches bicycling beside us seemed worried. Manfred Steffny, a German Olympic marathoner and organizer of the race, got irate as Christa and Manuela moved up on Judy's shoulder.

"You are going out too fast," he cried. "Don't you dare pass, stay right where you are."

Then, doing his best to be impartial because of the international nature of the marathon, he dropped back slightly to me and gave me a rundown on the positions and conditions of my teammates behind.

By five kilometers, Liane Winter, the German darkhorse running only her third marathon, obviously chafed under the moderate pace and surged past Judy and Marilyn into the lead. Most of us thought this reflected her inexperience and that she would tire, but it didn't turn out that way. Liane and Judy jockeyed for the lead over the next 15 kilometers, then Judy began to tire in the headwind while Christa and Chantal moved up. At about 37 kilometers, Liane took over the lead again from Chantal and held it to the end. She finished in 2:50:31, a new European record. Chantal was close behind in 2:51:45; Christa and Manuela finished third and fourth.

All this I learned after the fact, my experience of the race being limited to my own feelings and whatever I saw ahead of me. Feeling comfortable, I ran along steadily behind the lead pack. Right at the beginning, one disadvantage of the absence of men was clear. There were no large bodies to tuck in behind, to shelter us from that headwind. Furthermore, the small field quickly spread out, so that runners were alone for most of the race. Jacki Hansen, moving easily, was about one minute ahead of me throughout the race. And aside from the brief challenge from two German women between 10 and 20 kilometers, there was no one in sight behind me.

There was plenty of time to enjoy the course, half of it into the wind, but mostly past cheering crowds reminiscent of Boston, the other half on a bike path beside lovely woods, with a view of Waldniel and its church across the fields. We also ran past farms populated by clean but enormous swine. The local photographers loved to shoot views of us running past the sows—for contrast—I hope.

There were two aid stations on each loop, serviced by young local runners who would ask what we wanted, then sprint ahead to get it and run along with us while we drank. These girls had trouble pronouncing "ERG," speaking it more like "ugh." They considered it the American water and had plenty available. (Jacki and Peggy had brought supplies from the US.) We Americans amazed the Germans by drinking so much on the run. They seem to believe that chronic dehydration is easier on the system and that we would make ourselves sick.

No one got sick, but fatigue, the wind and perhaps (in Lucy's case) the herring began to take their toll of the Americans, most of whom slowed. Nina Kuscsik, who had paced with Jacki the first 20 kilometers, dropped back toward me and I passed her as we battled the wind. She tucked in behind but couldn't sustain the pace.

Personally, I was surprised she could run at all on Sunday.

Two days after our arrival in Europe, Judy and I had spent 14 hours in the sack and here was Nina out running. Amazing!

Shortly thereafter, around 27 kilometers, I passed Marilyn Paul. As Marilyn explains it, she felt a bit miffed at being passed by someone on 2:58 pace (having planned to run faster herself) and was provoked into speeding up for awhile. Before long, she tripped ("over my own feet") and fell, spraining a previously weakened ankle. As she hobbled on, feeling lonely, with the woods beside her and no one in sight front or rear, the overzealous German Red Cross in search of a victim drove by and abducted Marilyn into their ambulance over her loud protests of "Nein! Nein!" Viewing Marilyn's pronounced limp after the race, however, I had to agree with the Red Cross kidnappers.

Dr. van Aaken and his nephew Jochen were cruising around the course continually in a Mercedes equipped with a loudspeaker. They could be heard giving splits in English and calling encouragement to all of us. At 30 kilometers, the doctor informed me that Judy, too, was slowing and that I would eventually catch her if I kept on pace. I thought he was mixed up, since only Jacki Hansen was visible ahead of me and Jacki was obviously not slowing at all (she finished fifth overall and first American in a personal best of 2:56:25).

But sure enough, there shortly before 40 kilometers was Judy, worn out by the battle with the wind and Liane Winter. I passed her, secretly pleased that I, the sixth (and hitherto slowest) wheel on the AAU team, should finish first. One last turn into the headwind, another kilometer fighting it, and I finished sixth in 2:58:09, with Judy right behind me in 2:58:47.

There were seven women under three hours, a new record. There was a sizeable gap before the next bunch of runners began to come in, led by Nina Kuscsik in 3:06. Over half the finishers broke 3:30, though few, because of the wind, managed a PR. Ruth Anderson, who had hoped to regain the Masters world record by running 3:17, had been chilled and blown around like a leaf on the last lap. She ran 3:25.

Despite the personal disappointment for many, the mood at

Horst Muller

Americans (l-r) Anderson, Kuscsik, Paul, Ikenberry, Bunz and Ullyot are among the international leaders.

the finish was festive, even euphoric, helped by the obvious enthusiasm and warmth of the spectators and the townspeople of
Waldniel. Red Cross ladies flocked around us dispensing blan-
kets and hot tea. We had to explain to them, however, that we
were only tired, not dying. They kept trying to drag us off to

the field hospital, while we wanted to stay and watch the others finish.

The school children swarmed around again, continuing their autograph contest. TV stations begged for appropriate remarks in German ("Women's marathon in the Olympic Games" was considered appropriate) and looked (in vain) for a good set of newsworthy blisters to televise.

Dr. van Aaken, whose long-controversial views on the suitability of marathoning for women were so impressively vindicated, presided over the awards ceremonies and appeared much moved. He was not at all tired, however, and hosted a very *gemutlich* international party for runners and friends that evening in his house.

Liane Winter, the new champion, caught up with Marilyn and me as we limped gracefully off to the doctor's party, and we began chatting. She is a tall (5'10") woman of 32 who ran cross-country more than 10 years ago "when we were lucky to be allowed to run 900 meters across the grass." At that time, she was good enough to be part of the German champion team for four years.

Last year, after a long retirement, she took up distance running following the van Aaken training method. She ran her first marathon through snow and ice last February, in little over three hours. Her second, in May, was 2:57.

Liane's training is very simple: she runs once a day, in the evening after a full day's work, 20 kilometers one day over hills, a flat 30 kilometers the next. In the Waldniel marathon, she felt her size and strength gave her an advantage in the wind, which blew smaller women all over the place. And Liane did not worry that the early pace would tire her.

"I'm used to finishing strongly," she told me. On her 30-kilometer workouts, she runs the first 10 kilometers easy, the second 10 at moderate pace and bashes the last 10.

The party was a happy babble of voices—German, English, French. Sometime after 1 a.m., though there were still no signs of a lull in the festivities, Tom Sturak and I managed to get Dr. van Aaken off in a side room for an interview. With its leading light gone, the party slowly ground to a halt. By 3:30 a.m. when Tom and I, drooping with fatigue, had to terminate the interview, all was quiet in the other room.

Dr. van Aaken, having partied everyone under the table, was still full of energy and decided to read a while before retiring. We said good-bye with great reluctance, all of us surprised at the strength of the international friendships that had blossomed in those few days. We Americans will always, in the classic words of Jochen Gossenberger, "have a happy remembering of the little Willage of Waldniel."

sixteen

1975 "National"

New York City, site of the 1975 Women's National AAU Marathon Championship, is distinguished by freaky weather and a tough course—one small loop and four big ones—around Central Park. Natives of the city take a perverse pride in the hills and other assorted difficulties of their course.

"You may have run under 3:00 (or 2:30, 2:20 . . .) in Boston," they sneer, "but our course is much tougher."

They're right.

I reserved judgment on the course until after running it. But the freaky weather was apparent long before I got to New York. Leaving San Francisco on a balmy, clear September evening, I boarded a plane full of anxious New Yorkers.

This was Thursday, and they all were asking each other if last Sunday's rainstorm—the tail end of some hurricane—was still in progress. The answer was yes! Our pilot, obviously a black humorist, regaled us with periodic weather reports of torrential downpours, floods, heavy winds and the difficulties of flying—not to mention landing at Kennedy airport—under such adverse conditions.

We arrived safely nonetheless, in wind and rain, long after midnight. I was met by Nina Kuscsik, fourth in the 1974 championship but grounded this year by a back problem. Nina and Beth Bonner, back in 1971, had been the first women to run under three hours, and had done it at Central Park.

Several out-of-state runners called up during the night to ask if the race was still on. They had heard rumors that New York was floating out to sea.

During a temporary lull in the rainstorm the next day, Nina and I decided to run around the course. But by the time she had changed her clothes, the heavens had broken open again. So we drove. I was most impressed by the runners' lane, which was largely under water, and by the flair Nina showed in ignoring all the red lights along the six-mile drive.

"Oops, I keep forgetting I'm not running," she explained as she shot yet another light.

Saturday morning, the sun finally appeared. Nina went out for a 12-mile run while I puttered around the house and looked at the course description. It was not reassuring to read that the route would be "heavily patrolled at all times" by police and the Central Park bike squad. Now I could worry about muggers as well as hills, puddles and heat!

That evening, the West Side YMCA hosted a reception for the women runners and their friends. Two great vats of Hawaiian punch were set up, along with plates of rather horrible cookies. One vat was spiked with vodka, I learned much later, and shuddered as I realized how often we all dipped into it for refills.

Six of us were veterans of the 1975 Boston Marathon (including the first three American finishers—Kathy Switzer, Gayle Barron and Marilyn Bevans). However, I was startled to realize I was the only "holdover" from the previous year's National Championship in California. This lack of overlap was not solely because of geography. (There were four of us here from the West Coast, and a dozen states were represented.) I think it reflected instead the inevitable attrition among top competitors. Judy Ikenberry, last year's champion, was traveling in Europe, but many others were injured, or not in sufficiently good condition to justify the trip.

Ironically, for the second year in a row, the fastest American was unable to contest the championship. Jacki Hansen was just emerging from a period of exhaustion and bypassed the New York race. Two weeks later, closer to home, she set a new world record of 2:38:19.

Jacki's teammate, 40-year-old Miki Gorman, the female victor at Boston in 1974, did make the trip to New York and appeared at the reception with her usual entourage of husband Mike, a broad-shouldered handball player, and coach Lu Dosti. Miki was smiling, fit and trim (back to her usual 89 pounds)—eight months after the birth of her first child. This would be her "comeback" race.

A reporter innocently asked if Miki felt if she could run better after having a baby. "Oh yes!" laughed Miki, explaining that she had 20 hours of labor followed by a Caesarian. "Compared to having a baby, the marathon is easy. The pain is really nothing in a marathon."

I looked in vain for the darkhorse, Kim Merritt of Wisconsin, who had recently beaten Jacki Hansen in the Charleston 15-miler and was therefore my personal favorite to win the championship. We were all intimidated by rumors that Kim can run the mile in 4:52, trains with Lucian Rosa, and hoped to set a world record in this race—only her second marathon. But by the time we left for supper around 9 p.m., Kim had not yet appeared.

Sunday morning—race day—we drove in early to the city. The air was warm (by San Francisco standards), the skies clear, with no sign of the notorious New York smog—and alas, no sign of a cloud either. But the humidity was low, the course shaded and most of the puddles gone. It was a perfect day for spectators, and generally good for runners.

The good weather had brought New Yorkers to this park in droves, and the mood was festive at the starting line by Tavern-on-the-Green. Peanut and ice cream vendors, and press buses were prominent. Runners stretched and jogged in the shade, where it was still only 60 degrees but would warm up to 69 degrees during the race.

Lined up at the start, women (outnumbered 10-1 by the men), struggled to keep a toehold on our own section of front line, marked in red. Kathy Switzer bounced up in our midst and flashbulbs exploded wildly, as she was the odds-on local favorite. Kathy is the darling of the media. Her trademark racing

Gayle Barron of Georgia is the South's top woman marathoner and a friendly rival of Dr. Ullyot. Gayle finished third, Joan fourth in the 1975 AAU race, both breaking three hours.

garb is a short white dress set off by fluorescent green-and-yellow SL-76s and matching hair ribbons. Reporters and photographers swarmed around her before, during and after the race—a barrage of publicity which Kathy managed to handle graciously, even during the run.

Totally unheeded by the press, Kim Merritt appeared quickly on the front row of women just moments before the race. Then, after the usual-pre-race speeches, the gun went off and we all charged madly down the first slight incline, then squeezed together around a construction area. A few horses had preceded us in the "runners" lane, and some had left mementos of their passing. "Step in horse shit, it's good luck!" shouted one man as we all hopped and skipped around the piles.

The women were applauded loudly and Miki Gorman was reported to be "first" at two miles. Actually, Kim Merritt was already ahead of our bunch and had been overlooked as she flashed by in a group of men.

There was little jockeying for position among the women after an initial wild rush. Kim, 14-year-old Diane Barrett and Miki kept up the fast pace, while I eased off. Kathy Switzer moved off ahead, much to my relief, since she pulled along her press bus escort which had been honking loudly at cyclists and spewing exhaust fumes at all of us.

Somewhere behind me were the two best "pacers," Gayle Barron and Marilyn Bevans. Both like to start calmly and speed up as they run, catching more foolhardy competitors. They had breezed comfortably past me and many others at Boston this year, ending up third and fourth.

The first half of the race seemed very pleasant to me—as always. Later, the sun grew hotter, and the shade dwindled to nothing. Cyclists, pedestrians, dogs and horses cut across the runners' lane with increasing frequency—or perhaps they just were harder to dodge as I tired.

The hills grew perceptibly steeper on each lap. In fact, by the third time around I realized that the whole damn course was hilly. When it wasn't going up, it was weaving down and around a corner.

Around 17 miles, Gayle Barron caught up with me, looking fresh and bouncy. We exchanged a few words of encouragement—the typical "non-psych" of women marathoners, who generally take a real pleasure in each other's performances. But I couldn't match Gayle's faster pace, and soon lost sight of her. And altruism aside, I hoped Marilyn Bevans wouldn't pass me next, as she had at Boston. Alas, at 20 miles, there she was at my elbow—but apparently just as tired as I was. We stayed close together for several miles, alternating the lead at each aid station.

On the last rolling hill, I was surprised to overtake Diane Barrett, who had run hard with Kim Merritt for the first 15 miles, only to be done in by fatigue and the pace. By now she was pale and stumbling, her worried dad jogging beside her with a drink and a sponge, wondering if he should make her stop. But Diane gamely stayed on her feet that last mile and finished sixth in 3:01.

The finish, at last—endless yards past the starting line. I drank gallons of water and learned my time from Nina—2:58:30, close to my PR, and good for fourth place. We all stood around happily, exchanging stories of the race. Media interest in the women seemed high, or perhaps the reporters, too, were just enjoying the sunshine. In any case, whenever two of us met to exchange a few words, it seemed that a mike would pop up between us.

Among the bystanders who came over to compare notes was Diana Nyad, the same 25-year-old woman who had tried swimming around Manhattan a few days earlier. The top-ranked woman marathon swimmer in this country, Diane also had more than a passing interest in the Central Park marathon. She ran it herself the year before in 3:48.

I gradually pieced together the story of the race. The new women's champion was Kim Merritt, who kept up her fast early pace and ran 2:46:14—nine minutes under the women's course record, and seven minutes ahead of runner-up Miki Gorman.

Exhausted and shy, 20-year-old Kim eluded reporters at the finish, shook off the laurel wreath tossed over her head by an overzealous official as she crossed the line, and retreated alone to a distant park bench to recover. For this assertion of independence, she will probably become known as the Greta Garbo of long-distance running.

When the ceremonies finally got underway, Kim had to be hunted out again to receive her awards. She seemed overwhelmed by the applause, and disappeared again quickly. Miki Gorman, to her surprise, won the over-40 trophy—her first—in addition to second place overall. Miki's mark of 2:53:02 shattered the old world record of 3:12 for Masters women.

The comparison with the 1974 National AAU Championship in San Mateo—the first ever for women—was interesting. The 1975 field was smaller (44 starters, 36 finishers) and showed less depth (14 under 3:30, vs. 21 in 1974), reflecting the greater number of women marathoners on the West Coast.

However, speed among the top finishers had improved. Five of us broke three hours, and both Kim and Miki were under the 1974 winning time of 2:55. The actual improvement is probably far greater than times would indicate, since the San Mateo course of 1974 was completely flat. I was the only woman who competed in both races, and my time in 1975 was 15 minutes faster.

That night we caught the late news on TV and saw a few glimpses of the marathon—the crowded street; a shot of Kathy Switzer with ribbons and shoes flashing; Kim losing her laurel wreath as she finished. But the longest footage by far was devoted to a paunchy Central Park bench-warmer who wanted a ban on marathons in his quiet park.

"Look at all these crazy people!" he shouted angrily. "I bet they wouldn't run if they knew what happened to the first guy who ran a marathon—a Greek, who ran to Athens. That guy dropped dead!"

He implied that this fate was no more than Pheidippides deserved—not to mention all the kooks running in Central Park.

Appendix

BASIC FITNESS TEST

Dr. Kenneth Cooper devised the 1½-mile test of basic fitness for his Aerobics programs, which are described in his books *Aerobics, The New Aerobics* and *Aerobics for Women*. These are the 1½-mile time categories for women, with allowances for age differences.

Category	Below age 30	Ages 30-39	Ages 40-49	Ages 50-up
Very poor	above 17:30	above 18:30	above 18:30	above 20:30
Poor	15:31-17:30	16:31-18:30	17:31-19:30	18:31-20:30
Fair	13:31-15:30	14:31-16:30	15:31-17:30	16:31-18:30
Good	11:01-13:30	11:31-14:30	12:31-15:30	13:31-16:30
Excellent	below 11:00	below 11:30	below 12:30	below 13:30

WOMEN'S TIME STANDARDS

The Road Runners Club of America sponsors a nationwide awards program for both men and women. Ken Young devised the standards, based on his studies of racing performances, and the RRCA recognizes runners who better the marks in races which meet certain qualifications of sanction and distance. The standards for women:

Event	World-Class	Champion	Class A	Class B	Class C
6 miles	33:00	35:30	38:00	41:30	45:30
10 kilometers	34:00	36:30	39:30	43:00	47:00
15 kilometers	52:30	56:00	1:00:30	1:06:00	1:12:00
10 miles	56:30	1:00:30	1:05:00	1:11:00	1:17:30
One hour	10m 1100y	9m 1600y	9m 400y	8m 900y	7m 1500y
20 kilometers	1:11:00	1:16:00	1:22:00	1:29:00	1:37:30
15 miles	1:26:30	1:33:00	1:40:00	1:49:00	1:59:30
25 kilometers	1:29:30	1:36:30	1:44:00	1:53:00	2:04:00
30 kilometers	1:49:00	1:57:00	2:06:30	2:18:00	2:31:00
20 miles	1:57:30	2:06:30	2:16:30	2:28:30	2:43:00
Marathon	2:38:00	2:50:00	3:04:00	3:20:00	3:39:30
50 kilometers	3:10:30	3:25:00	3:41:30	4:01:30	4:25:30

RACE PACING TABLES

Proper pacing is of vital importance in long-distance racing, and even pacing generally produces the best results. The chart below indicates. The chart below serves two purposes: (1) It tells what a certain pace per mile will yield in terms of overall time. For instance, two hours for 20 miles is 8:00 per mile; (2) It shows how to pace evenly. A runner trying for 3:30 in the marathon might go through five miles in 40 minutes, 10 in 1:20 and so on.

Since races increasingly are run at metric distances, we include metric conversion and pacing tables on pages 152 and 153.

Mile	5 Miles	10 Miles	15 Miles	20 Miles	Marathon	50 Miles
4:50	24:10	48:20	1:12:30	1:36:40	2:07:44	
5:30	27:30	55:00	1:22:30	1:50:00	2:24:12	
5:40	28:20	56:40	1:25:00	1:53:20	2:28:34	
5:50	29:10	58:20	1:27:30	1:56:40	2:32:56	
6:00	30:00	1:00:00	1:30:00	2:00:00	2:37:19	5:00:00
6:10	30:50	1:01:40	1:32:30	2:03:20	2:41:41	5:08:20
6:20	31:40	1:03:20	1:35:00	2:06:40	2:46:03	5:16:40
6:30	32:30	1:05:00	1:37:30	2:10:00	2:50:25	5:25:00
6:40	33:20	1:06:40	1:40:00	2:13:20	2:54:47	5:33:20
6:50	34:10	1:08:20	1:42:30	2:16:40	2:59:09	5:41:40
7:00	35:00	1:10:00	1:45:00	2:20:00	3:03:33	5:50:00
7:10	35:00	1:11:40	1:18:20	2:23:20	3:07:55	5:58:20
7:20	36:40	1:13:20	1:50:00	2:26:40	3:12:17	6:06:40
7:30	37:30	1:15:00	1:52:30	2:30:00	3:16:39	6:15:00
7:40	38:20	1:16:40	1:55:00	2:33:20	3:21:01	6:23:20
7:50	39:10	1:18:20	1:57:30	2:36:40	3:25:23	6:31:40
8:00	40:00	1:20:00	2:00:00	2:40:00	3:29:45	6:40:00
8:10	40:50	1:21:40	2:02:30	2:43:20	3:34:07	6:48:20
8:20	41:40	1:23:20	2:05:00	2:46:40	3:38:29	6:56:40
8:30	42:30	1:25:00	2:07:30	2:50:00	3:42:51	7:05:00
8:40	43:20	1:26:40	2:10:00	2:53:20	3:47:13	7:13:20
8:50	44:10	1:28:20	2:12:30	2:56:40	3:51:35	7:21:40
9:00	45:00	1:30:00	2:15:00	3:00:00	3:56:00	7:30:00
9:10	45:50	1:31:40	2:17:30	3:03:20	4:00:22	7:38:20
9:20	46:40	1:33:20	2:20:00	3:06:40	4:04:44	7:46:40
9:30	47:30	1:35:00	2:22:30	3:10:00	4:09:06	7:55:00
9:40	48:20	1:36:40	2:25:00	3:13:20	4:13:28	8:03:20
9:50	49:10	1:38:20	2:27:30	3:16:40	4:17:50	8:11:40

MILE-METER CONVERSIONS

(NOTE: A kilometer is 1000 meters)

50 meters = 54 yards 6.5 inches
60 meters = 65 yards 1 foot 10.2 inches
100 meters = 109 yards 1 foot 1 inch
110 meters = 120 yards 10.7 inches
200 meters = 218 yards 2 feet 2 inches
300 meters = 328 yards 3 inches
400 meters = 437 yards 1 foot 4 inches
500 meters = 546 yards 2 feet 5 inches
600 meters = 656 yards 6 inches
800 meters = 874 yards 2 feet 8 inches
1000 meters = 1093 yards 1 foot 10 inches
1500 meters = 1640 yards 1 foot 3 inches
2000 meters = 1 mile 427 yards 8 inches
3000 meters = 1 mile 1520 yards 2 feet 6 inches
4000 meters = 2 miles 854 yards 1 foot 4 inches
5000 meters = 3 miles 188 yards 2.4 inches
6000 meters = 3 miles 1281 yards 2 feet
7000 meters = 4 miles 615 yards 10 inches
8000 meters = 4 miles 1708 yards 2 feet 8 inches
9000 meters = 5 miles 1042 yards 1 foot 6 inches
10,000 meters = 6 miles 376 yards 4.8 inches
12,000 meters = 7 miles 803 yards 1 foot
15,000 meters = 9 miles 564 yards 7.2 inches
20,000 meters = 12 miles 752 yards 9.6 inches
25,000 meters = 15 miles 940 yards 1 foot
30,000 meters = 18 miles 1128 yards 1 foot 2.4 inches
35,000 meters = 21 miles 1316 yards 1 foot 4.8 inches
40,000 meters = 24 miles 1504 yards 1 foot 7.2 inches
50,000 meters = 31 miles 120 yards 2 feet
60,000 meters = 37 miles 476 yards 2 feet 4.8 inches
70,000 meters = 43 miles 872 yards 2 feet 9.6 inches
80,000 meters = 49 miles 1249 yards 2.4 inches
90,000 meters = 55 miles, 1625 yards 7.2 inches
100,000 meters = 62 miles 241 yards 1 foot

50 yards = 45.72m
60 yards = 54.864m
70 yards = 64.008m
100 yards = 91.44m
120 yards = 109.728
220 yards = 201.168
300 yards = 274.32m
330 yards = 301.644
440 yards = 402.336
500 yards = 457.2m
600 yards = 548.64m
660 yards = 603.504
880 yards = 804.672
1000 yards = 914.4m
1320 yards = 1207.0
One mile = 1609.344
2 miles = 3218.688m
3 miles = 4828.032m
4 miles = 6437.376m
5 miles = 8046.72m
6 miles = 9656.064m
7 miles = 11,265.408
8 miles = 12,874.752
9 miles = 14,484.096
10 miles = 16,093.44
15 miles = 24,140.16
20 miles = 32,186.88
Marathon = 42,195m
30 miles = 48,280.32
40 miles = 64,373.76
50 miles = 80,467.2m
60 miles = 96,560.64
70 miles = 112,654.0
80 miles = 128,747.5
90 miles = 144,840.9
100 miles = 160,934.

MILE-KILOMETER TIME COMPARISONS

Mile	Kilometer	Mile	Kilometer
4:00	2:29.16	7:00	4:21.03
4:10	2:35.37	7:10	4:27.24
4:20	2:41.59	7:20	4:33.46
4:30	2:47.80	7:30	4:39.67
4:40	2:54.02	7:40	4:45.89
4:50	3:00.23	7:50	4:52.10
5:00	3:06.45	8:00	4:58.32
5:10	3:12.66	8:10	5:04.53
5:20	3:18.88	8:20	5:10.75
5:30	3:25.09	8:30	5:16.96
5:40	3:31.31	8:40	5:23.18
5:50	3:37.52	8:50	5:29.39
6:00	3:43.74	9:00	5:35.61
6:10	3:49.95	9:10	5:41.82
6:20	3:56.17	9:20	5:48.04
6:30	4:02.38	9:30	5:54.25
6:40	4:08.60	9:40	6:00.47
6:50	4:14.81	9:50	6:06.68

METRIC PACING TABLES

1 Km.	10 Kms.	15 Kms.	20 Kms.	25 Kms.	30 Kms.	50 Kms.
3:00	30:00	45:00	1:00:00	1:15:00	1:30:00	2:30:00
3:10	31:40	47:30	1:03:20	1:19:10	1:35:00	2:38:20
3:20	33:20	50:00	1:06:40	1:23:20	1:40:00	2:46:40
3:30	35:00	52:30	1:10:00	1:27:30	1:45:00	2:55:00
3:40	36:40	55:00	1:13:20	1:31:40	1:50:00	3:03:20
3:50	38:20	57:30	1:16:40	1:35:50	1:55:00	3:11:40
4:00	40:00	1:00:00	1:20:00	1:40:00	2:00:00	3:20:00
4:10	41:40	1:02:30	1:23:20	1:44:10	2:05:00	3:28:20
4:20	43:20	1:05:00	1:26:40	1:48:20	2:10:00	3:36:40
4:30	45:00	1:07:30	1:30:00	1:52:30	2:15:00	3:45:00
4:40	46:40	1:10:00	1:33:20	1:56:40	2:20:00	3:53:20
4:50	48:20	1:12:30	1:36:40	2:00:50	2:25:00	4:01:40
5:00	50:00	1:15:00	1:40:00	2:05:00	2:30:00	4:10:00
5:10	51:40	1:17:30	1:43:20	2:09:10	2:35:00	4:18:20
5:20	53:20	1:20:00	1:46:40	2:13:20	2:40:00	4:26:40
5:30	55:00	1:22:30	1:50:00	2:17:30	2:45:00	4:35:00
5:40	56:40	1:25:00	1:53:20	2:21:40	2:50:00	4:43:20
5:50	58:20	1:27:30	1:56:40	2:25:50	2:55:00	4:51:40

Recommended Reading

BOOKS

- *Aerobics for Women*, by Kenneth Cooper, M.D., and Mildred Cooper
- *The Complete Runner*, from the editors of *RW*.
- *Dr. Sheehan on Running*, by George Sheehan, M.D.
- *Guide to Distance Running*, from the editors of *RW*.
- *The Long-Run Solution*, by Joe Henderson.
- *The New Aerobics*, by Kenneth Cooper, M.D.
- *Run to the Top*, by Arthur Lydiard.
- *On the Run from Dogs and People*, by Hal Higdon.
- *The Self-Made Olympian*, by Ron Daws.
- *The Van Aaken Method*, by Ernst van Aaken, M.D.

BOOKLETS

- *Beginning Running*, from the editors of *Runner's World*.
- *The Conditioning of Distance Runners*, by Tom Osler.
- *Exercises for Runners*, from the editors of *RW*.
- *Long Slow Distance*, by Joe Henderson.
- *Run Gently Run Long*, by Joe Henderson.
- *The Runner's Diet*, from the editors of *RW*.
- *Runner's Training Guide*, from the editors of *RW*.
- *The Running Body*, by E.C. Frederick

All publications except *Run to the Top* and *On the Run from Dogs and People* (out of print) are available from World Publications, Box 366, Mountain View, Calif. 94040. Write to the company for current price information.

About the Author

Ron Daws

Joan Ullyot attended Wellesley College and the Free University of Berlin, and is a graduate of the Harvard Medical School. Dr. Ullyot's running has led her to change her medical specialty from pathology to exercise physiology, and she has directed the Aerobics and Physiology Division of the Institute of Health Research in San Francisco. One of her projects there has been to develop programs for beginning runners, both men and women, and to monitor their progress.

Born in 1940, Dr. Ullyot did not begin running until the early 1970s. She ran her first marathon in 1973. The next year, competed in the first US women's marathon championship and the first world race. Dr. Ullyot finished sixth in the latter race and fourth in the 1975 US championship. She has run 2:51:15 for the marathon, and she holds the women's record for the Pike's Peak Marathon. She runs with the West Valley Track Club.

Joan lives in San Francisco with her two sons, Teddy and Jonathan.